New Directions for
Teaching and Learning

Marilla D. Svinicki
EDITOR-IN-CHIEF

R. Eugene Rice
CONSULTING EDITOR

Educating Integrated Professionals:
Theory and Practice on Preparation for the Professoriate

Carol L. Colbeck
KerryAnn O'Meara
Ann E. Austin
EDITORS

Number 113 • Spring 2008
Jossey-Bass
San Francisco

EDUCATING INTEGRATED PROFESSIONALS: THEORY AND PRACTICE ON
PREPARATION FOR THE PROFESSORIATE
Carol L. Colbeck, KerryAnn O'Meara, Ann E. Austin (eds.)
New Directions for Teaching and Learning, no. 113
Marilla D. Svinicki, Editor-in-Chief
R. Eugene Rice, Consulting Editor

Microfilm copies of issues and articles are available in 16mm and 35mm,
as well as microfiche in 105mm, through University Microfilms, Inc.,
300 North Zeeb Road, Ann Arbor, Michigan 48106-1346.

NEW DIRECTIONS FOR TEACHING AND LEARNING (ISSN 0271-0633, electronic ISSN 1536-0768) is part of The Jossey-Bass Higher and Adult
Education Series and is published quarterly by Wiley Subscription Services, Inc., A Wiley Company, at Jossey-Bass, 989 Market Street, San
Francisco, California 94103-1741. Periodicals postage paid at San Francisco, California, and at additional mailing offices. POSTMASTER: Send
address changes to New Directions for Teaching and Learning, Jossey-
Bass, 989 Market Street, San Francisco, California 94103-1741.

New Directions for Teaching and Learning is indexed in CIJE: Current
Index to Journals in Education (ERIC), Contents Pages in Education
(T&F), Current Abstracts (EBSCO), Educational Research Abstracts
Online (T&F), ERIC Database (Education Resources Information Cen-
ter), Higher Education Abstracts (Claremont Graduate University), and
SCOPUS (Elsevier).

SUBSCRIPTIONS cost $85 for individuals and $209 for institutions, agencies,
and libraries in the United States. Prices subject to change. See order form
at end of book.

EDITORIAL CORRESPONDENCE should be sent to the editor-in-chief, Marilla
D. Svinicki, Department of Educational Psychology, University of Texas
at Austin, One University Station, D5800, Austin, TX 78712.

www.josseybass.com

CONTENTS

EDITORS' NOTES
KerryAnn O'Meara, Carol L. Colbeck, Ann E. Austin

1. Professional Identity Development Theory and Doctoral   9
Education
Carol L. Colbeck
Doctoral education should prepare future faculty to integrate their professional identities as researchers, teachers, and providers of community service.

2. Applying Lessons from Professional Education to the   17
Preparation of the Professoriate
Chris M. Golde
Lessons learned from education for the professions illustrates how to prepare future professors to become stewards of their disciplines' knowledge, skills, and values.

3. Graduate Education and Community Engagement   27
KerryAnn O'Meara
This chapter uses socialization theory to explore how to integrate community engagement throughout doctoral education.

4. Networking to Develop a Professional Identity: A Look at   43
the First-Semester Experience of Doctoral Students in Business
Vicki L. Sweitzer
This empirical study shows how messages from faculty, peers, and family influenced the professional identity development of business students during their first year of doctoral study.

5. Lost in Translation: Learning Professional Roles Through   57
the Situated Curriculum
Emily M. Janke, Carol L. Colbeck
Curricular theories informed this study of how a teaching assistant preparation program in chemistry unintentionally interfered with research-teaching integration.

6. Strategies for Preparing Integrated Faculty: The Center for   69
the Integration of Research, Teaching, and Learning
Ann E. Austin, Mark R. Connolly, Carol L. Colbeck
A comprehensive program prepares science, technology, engineering, and mathematics (STEM) doctoral students for faculty careers that integrate research and education.

7. Career Preparation for Doctoral Students: The University of   83
Kansas History Department
Eve Levin
A history department reformed its graduate program to prepare stu-
dents for their professional academic careers.

Concluding Thoughts   99
Carol L. Colbeck, KerryAnn O'Meara, Ann E. Austin

INDEX   103

EDITORS' NOTES

Succeeding generations of college and university faculty are prepared in doctoral programs. Most arts and sciences doctoral students want academic careers (Golde and Dore, 2001), and a majority of those who complete doctoral degrees in the United States find immediate employment or engage in postdoctoral study in U.S. colleges and universities (Hoffer and others, 2006). These new faculty are unlikely to feel adequately prepared for their new jobs. Doctoral students say they learn how to conduct research but not how to publish or secure grants. They are getting practice at running recitation or laboratory sections but not in lecturing, conducting discussions, engaging students in active learning, or advising. Their doctoral programs provide them few opportunities to participate in governance or in community service (Gaff, Pruitt-Logan, and Weibl, 2000; Golde and Dore, 2001). National programs such as Preparing Future Faculty (PFF), the Carnegie Initiative on the Doctorate (CID), the Alliance for Graduate Education and the Professoriate (AGEP), and independent university and department programs are trying to address these deficiencies by preparing doctoral students to be effective teachers, to conduct research with undergraduates or in resource-poor environments, and to be ready to engage in governance (Adams, 2002).

While these reform efforts are well intentioned, to the extent that they focus on research, teaching, and service as separate elements of academic work, many remedies for doctoral education actually preserve what Eugene Rice (1986) labeled the "older academic professional model" that assumes "bifurcation" of teaching and research and may neglect community service altogether. This approach may actually lead to deprofessionalization of faculty work, subdividing it into tasks subject to formal coordination and management by administrators (Rhoades, 1998).

In contrast, an integrated approach to faculty work—and to doctoral education—assumes that faculty are highly qualified, flexible, and complex workers who can handle nonroutine work and see how different aspects of their professional work inform the other various aspects (Scott, 2003). This volume therefore focuses on educating future faculty to integrate their work in two interrelated ways. The first emphasizes synergy among teaching, research, and service roles, thereby encouraging current and future faculty to "enrich their teaching with their research, inform their research with lessons learned from community service, and engage in public scholarship that integrates teaching, research, and service" (Colbeck, 2002, p. 44). The second emphasizes connections between professional and academic aspects of faculty work. The mathematician Hyman Bass, for example, considers his

NEW DIRECTIONS FOR TEACHING AND LEARNING, no. 113, Spring 2008   © Wiley Periodicals, Inc.
Published online in Wiley InterScience (www.interscience.wiley.com) • DOI: 10.1002/tl.303

field both a *discipline,* with an associated domain of knowledge, methods, and understandings, and a *profession*—"an intellectual community dedicated to knowledge generation, application, conservation, and transmission" interacting with other disciplines, institutions, and society (2006, p. 102). Faculty members who integrate their disciplinary and professional work are adept at recognizing and solving ill-defined problems, skilled at understanding and responding to ethical questions inherent in the various aspects of their work, and able to discover, teach, and apply knowledge with colleagues, students, and community partners in a variety of ways.

We expect this volume to be useful and to provoke discussion among faculty, graduate program directors, and deans charged with stewarding doctoral programs; scholars who study graduate education; and doctoral students themselves. Their interest in improving education for the professoriate is high for several reasons, including new pressures from the globalization of academic work, changing faculty appointments, and a renewed emphasis on the public responsibility of the academy.

Changing Contexts of Academic Work

Academic work is increasingly global—and therefore complex, challenging, and competitive. At the same time, colleges and universities are fragmenting the work of the academy by dividing labor among different professionals and paraprofessionals. While bureaucratic division of labor may enhance the economic competitiveness of individual colleges or universities, it may also reduce their effectiveness in serving the public good.

Universities in the United States prepare American and international students for positions in colleges and universities throughout the world. The international context for educating future faculty as innovative, competitive, skilled professionals fosters a focus on ensuring excellence in the selection, retention, and forward-looking education of doctoral students. A recent report from the Council of Graduate School's Advisory Committee on Graduate Education and American Competitiveness asserts that U.S. graduate education should "ensure that the knowledge creators and innovators of tomorrow have the cultural awareness, skills, and expertise to compete effectively in a knowledge-based economy" (2007, p. 1). Many of the report's recommendations point toward integration of academic work and assert that graduate programs should accomplish the following:

- Urge students to become citizen-scholars who use their knowledge and skills in real-world settings, gaining scholarly experience through service to community, state, nation, and the world (integration of research and community engagement)
- Provide exposure to the array of roles and responsibilities that constitute the professoriate of the twenty-first century (integration of teaching, research, community engagement, and administrative service)

NEW DIRECTIONS FOR TEACHING AND LEARNING • DOI: 10.1002/tl

• Reward creativity and risk-taking as key components of a U.S. strategy for innovation (integration of academic skills with professional orientations and values)

The report states that national economic competitiveness depends on a "creative class of knowledge workers who exhibit not just the mastery of a subject area, but the creative ability and drive to reshape the boundaries of knowledge and navigate between geo-cultural boundaries" (p. 5). The Council argues for reforms that make future academic professionals more agile, creative, responsive to the needs of society, collaborative, interdisciplinary, and adept at contributing to the public good.

Reformers may wish future faculty—individually and collectively—to demonstrate creativity, intercultural sensitivity, responsiveness, and innovation, but a "massive makeover" in the academic profession (Schuster and Finkelstein, 2006, p. 54) may inhibit rather than encourage integrated professional approaches to academic work. Nearly two in five full-time instructional staff in U.S. colleges and universities now hold term-limited appointments subject to renewal (Schuster and Finkelstein, 2006). While the trend is to create academic positions focused solely on teaching, research, or outreach, we argue that academic work will be impoverished if most faculty do not have the skills and capacity to make connections across academic and professional roles and responsibilities. Future faculty should be prepared with the skills and desire to find and foster connections between their research, teaching, and service through—or despite—their appointment role assignments.

This role integration is particularly important within a cultural context that is paying ever more attention to professionals' responsibility to serve the public good. William Sullivan (2005) described the social compact made between most professions and the public. In exchange for their autonomy and privilege, professionals will serve society in ways that go beyond economic development. Faculty members who are "professional" in this sense may not abdicate their academic responsibilities for participating in shared institutional governance, for sharing as well as discovering knowledge, for relating knowledge to public issues and to other disciplines, or for mentoring new professionals. The future of the professoriate, at least in the eyes of the public, lies in embracing public responsibilities and viewing academic work through the lenses of the stakeholders they serve, thereby orienting integrated professional work toward public purposes.

Overview of Chapters

The chapters in this volume use several theoretical lenses to improve understanding of the professional identity development process of doctoral students, the current preparation of future faculty, and new ways to educate doctoral students who will be ready to begin their faculty positions as professionals who integrate teaching, research, and service. Most of the theory-based research on doctoral preparation for faculty careers to date uses socialization theory, which has much to offer those who think about how new graduate students are prepared for academic life. In addition to socialization theory, our authors draw on theories of identity development, professional apprenticeship, mentoring, social networks, situated curriculum, concurrent curricula, and academic planning to illuminate some of the drawbacks of current education for the professoriate and point toward possibilities for improving practice in this area.

The first three chapters feature innovative applications of theory for understanding the possibilities of educating future faculty as integrated professionals. In Chapter One, Carol L. Colbeck draws on professionalization and identity development theories as foundational for viewing academic work as an integrated whole rather than an uneasy amalgam of disjointed research, teaching, and service roles. The silent revolution in faculty appointments (Schuster and Finkelstein, 2006) has already begun to fragment faculty roles into separately appointed teaching, research, or public service positions. Educating doctoral students to embrace the complexity and connectivity of all academic roles may help "reprofessionalize" faculty work for future generations.

Chris M. Golde was at the forefront of one of the best-known efforts to reform doctoral programs at the Carnegie Foundation. In Chapter Two, she considers how a theory of professional apprenticeship derived from preparation of lawyers, doctors, engineers, nurses, and the clergy might inform doctoral education. Building from the work of William Sullivan (Sullivan, 2005), Golde describes three apprenticeships in which doctoral students should engage: an intellectual apprenticeship to gain knowledge of a field, an apprenticeship of skills learned in practice, and a values apprenticeship centered in ethics of the profession.

Socialization theory provides the lens for exploring how to weave the much neglected but increasingly important and relevant faculty role of engaged scholar into doctoral preparation. In Chapter Three, KerryAnn O'Meara considers the knowledge and understandings, skills, and professional orientations (Austin and McDaniels, 2006) that future engaged scholars might acquire during the four stages of socialization of their doctoral experience. O'Meara imagines how graduate programs might attract and orient future faculty toward community engagement through targeted recruitment, funding, mentoring, practice, and curricular structures.

The next two chapters use theory to inform case study research about current doctoral preparation in two specific graduate programs. Chapters Four and Five provide vivid examples of how current practices in doctoral education may foster fragmentation and deprofessionalization of academic work. Their findings are similar, even though one chapter focuses on business and the other on chemistry and the authors use different theoretical frameworks. These chapters draw on lessons learned from the case studies to offer positive alternatives for educating doctoral students as integ... professionals.

In Chapter Four, Vicki L. Sweitzer explores experiences of doctoral students in a business program ranked among the top fifty in the United States. Sweitzer's conceptual framework combined theories of mentoring, social networks, and professional identity to understand how messages from peers, family, and friends, in addition to advisors and faculty, influenced professional identity development of twelve first-year doctoral students. She found that even at the end of the first semester in their programs, the composition of students' support networks and the nature of the support network partners provided were beginning to shape students' perceptions that professional identity should either be fragmented (focused solely on research) or integrated (incorporating research, teaching, and service).

Chemistry was the site and curricular theories the lens for Emily M. Janke and Carol L. Colbeck's case study of formal professional development training for new doctoral students. Their case study, described in Chapter Five, used theories of the college curriculum as academic plan, concurrent curricula, and the situated curriculum to explore how doctoral preparation shapes graduate students' perceptions of academic work along a continuum from integrated to fragmented. They found that the social and organizational contexts of learning are particularly profound for organizational newcomers such as doctoral students because through interactions, observations, sequencing of tasks, and responsibility assignments, newcomers learn what to know and who to be as a developing professional.

Examples of current efforts to educate doctoral students as integrated professionals are described in the next two chapters. In Chapter Six, Ann E. Austin, Mark R. Connolly, and Carol L. Colbeck describe a project funded by the National Science Foundation called the Center for the Integration of Research, Teaching, and Learning (CIRTL). Scholar-educators from science, technology, engineering, and math (STEM) disciplines have been working together with social scientists at several research universities to develop, implement, and evaluate tools, strategies, and programs to encourage doctoral students to apply their research skills to continuous improvement of their teaching and their students' learning. Here the focus is on preparing professors who integrate their research and teaching.

Integration of professional with academic apprenticeships for doctoral preparation of historians is the focus of Chapter Seven. Eve Levin describes how the University of Kansas history department reformed its doctoral program in association with the Carnegie Initiative of the Doctorate. With very little funding, the department identified strengths and weaknesses in a self-study and then implemented carefully crafted plans to prepare doctoral students as integrated professionals and what the Carnegie Foundation calls "stewards of the discipline," ready for the range of roles and contexts in which they would do their work.

Finally, in Concluding Thoughts, we consider lessons learned from each of the chapters about transforming doctoral education to prepare future faculty as integrated professionals.

KerryAnn O'Meara
Carol L. Colbeck
Ann E. Austin
Editors

References

Adams, K. A. *What Colleges and Universities Want in New Faculty.* Preparing Future Faculty Occasional Paper no. 8. Washington, D.C.: Association of American Colleges and Universities, 2002.

Austin, A. E., and McDaniels, M. "Using Doctoral Education to Prepare Faculty to Work Within Boyer's Four Domains of Scholarship." In J. M. Braxton (ed.), *Analyzing Faculty Work and Rewards: Using Boyer's Four Domains of Scholarship.* New Directions for Institutional Research, no. 129. San Francisco: Jossey-Bass, 2006.

Bass, H. "Developing Scholars and Professionals." In C. M. Golde and G. E. Walker (eds.), *Envisioning the Future of Doctoral Education: Preparing Stewards of the Discipline.* San Francisco: Jossey-Bass, 2006.

Colbeck, C. L. "Integration: Evaluating Faculty Work as a Whole." In C. L. Colbeck (ed.), *Evaluating Faculty Performance.* New Directions for Institutional Research, no. 114. San Francisco: Jossey-Bass, 2002.

Council of Graduate Schools Advisory Committee on Graduate Education and American Competitiveness. *Graduate Education: The Backbone of American Competitiveness and Innovation.* Washington, D.C.: Council of Graduate Schools, 2007.

Gaff, J. G., Pruitt-Logan, A. S., and Weibl, R. A. *Building the Faculty We Need: Colleges and Universities Working Together.* Washington, D.C.: Association of American Colleges and Universities, 2000.

Golde, C. M., and Dore, T. M. *At Cross Purposes: What the Experiences of Doctoral Students Reveal About Doctoral Education.* Philadelphia: Pew Charitable Trusts, 2001.

Hoffer, T. B., and others. *Doctorate Recipients from United States Universities: Summary Report, 2005.* Chicago: National Opinion Research Center, 2006.

Rhoades, G. *Managed Professionals: Unionized Faculty and Restructuring Academic Labor.* Albany: State University of New York Press, 1998.

Rice, R. E. "The Academic Profession in Transition: Toward a New Social Fiction." *Teaching Sociology,* 1986, *14,* 12–13.

Schuster, J. H., and Finkelstein, M. J. *The American Faculty: The Restructuring of Academic Work and Careers.* Baltimore: Johns Hopkins University Press, 2006.

Scott, W. R. *Organizations: Rational, Natural, and Open Systems.* (5th ed.) Upper Saddle River, N.J.: Prentice Hall, 2003.

Sullivan, W. M. *Work and Integrity. The Crisis and Promise of Professionalism in America.* (2nd ed.) San Francisco: Jossey-Bass, 2005.

KERRYANN O'MEARA *is associate professor of higher education at the University of Maryland at College Park. Her research focuses on the ways in which we socialize, reward, and support the growth of faculty so that they can make distinct contributions to the goals of higher education.*

CAROL L. COLBECK *is professor and dean of education at the University of Massachusetts in Boston. Her research investigates how faculty integrate teaching, research, and service; how faculty teaching and organizational climate affect student learning; and how faculty balance professional and personal responsibilities.*

ANN E. AUSTIN *holds the Dr. Mildred B. Erickson Distinguished Chair in Higher, Adult, and Lifelong Education at Michigan State University. Her research focuses on faculty careers and professional development, the preparation of future faculty, teaching and learning issues, academic workplaces, and organizational change and transformation in higher education.*

1

This chapter explores the benefits of enhancing doctoral students' abilities to exploit the synergies among their multiple academic identities.

Professional Identity Development Theory and Doctoral Education

Carol L. Colbeck

The academic profession is among a limited number of occupations that have attained the professional status associated with comparatively high levels of prestige, monetary rewards, security, and autonomy. Traits that most professions have in common include a specialized body of knowledge that supports the skills needed to practice the profession, a culture sustained by a professional association, an ethical code for professional practice, recognized authority based on exclusive expertise, and an imperative to serve the public responsibly (Greenwood, 1957; Silva, 2000).

Students learn their chosen profession's abstract body of professional knowledge and its associated skills during lengthy degree programs and apprenticeships. Students also observe the behaviors, attitudes, and norms for social interaction prevalent among practitioners of their profession. They interpret their observations in light of their own prior experiences, their goals for the future, and their current sense of who they are and will try on possible professional selves to see how well they fit (Ibarra, 1999). In the process, each student is crafting a sense of identity as a particular type of professional. The period of doctoral preparation is particularly important because although identity is resistant to change, adaptations to one's sense of self are more likely to occur when one is transitioning to a new role (Cast, 2003; Ibarra, 1999). According to Austin and McDaniels (2006), developing an identity as a professional scholar is an essential task for a doctoral student.

NEW DIRECTIONS FOR TEACHING AND LEARNING, no. 113, Spring 2008   © Wiley Periodicals, Inc.
Published online in Wiley InterScience (www.interscience.wiley.com) • DOI: 10.1002/tl.304

In this chapter, I use identity and professionalization theories to explore how doctoral students develop identities as professionals and how their educational contexts shape the nature of their professional identities as integrated or fragmented. I also discuss the implications of integrated or fragmented identities for their future careers as faculty members as well as for the academic profession as a whole.

Identity Theory

Identity is "what it means to be who one is" (Burke, 2003a, p. 1), and individuals' identities are often associated with labels for social positions or roles. Role labels convey meanings and expectations for behavior that have evolved from countless interactions among people in a social system. In a research university setting, for example, the role labels "sophomore," "first-year doctoral student," "teaching assistant," "postdoc," "new assistant professor," "chemist," and "writing specialist" instantly convey varying sets of expectations for how much time the individuals filling these roles will spend in the library, lab, or office and the number and nature of their interactions with freshmen, doctoral students, or tenured faculty members.

Roles are externally defined by other's expectations, but individuals define their own identities internally as they accept or reject social role expectations as part of who they are (Stryker and Burke, 2000). Once an individual has accepted and internalized expectations for a role as part of his or her identity, that identity becomes a cognitive framework for interpreting new experiences. For example, a first-year doctoral student who had spent much time and effort negotiating admission to a prestigious biochemistry program and is trying on the possible identity of serious scholar may be more likely to feel her professional identity validated by a professor's invitation to a research colloquium than by another student's invitation to a workshop on effective teaching.

Multiple Identities. On the other hand, this doctoral student may face some identity challenges if she began her doctoral program with an already established identity as a dedicated high school biology teacher. People live and work within many social networks. Individuals may have as many identities as the number of groups within which they engage in distinctive roles (Stryker and Burke, 2000). According to Stryker (1968), individuals organize their identities in a hierarchy that affects the likelihood that one identity will be more salient than other identities in any given situation. If the teaching workshop and the research colloquium are on different days, the doctoral student may accept invitations to both activities; her existing teacher identity will be activated at the first event and her emerging research identity at the second.

When two identities with contrasting meanings and expectations are activated at the same time, an individual is likely to experience stress. In our example, the doctoral student might feel stressed if the colloquium and the workshop are scheduled during the same time period. To further explore how individuals cope with identity conflicts, assume that the new doctoral student receives the invitations to the research colloquium and the teaching workshop during the same informal conversation with faculty and peers after a graduate student orientation event.

According to Stryker's articulation of identity theory, the student will decide in favor of the identity most salient to her (Stryker, 1968; Stryker and Burke, 2000). Salience will be determined by her level of commitment to each identity. Commitment, in turn, is shaped by the extensiveness or number of social connections or role partners one has in relation to an identity and the intensiveness or depth of those relationships with role partners. She may well decide to go to the research colloquium if the teaching role partner extending the workshop invitation is a new student from a humanities program whom she has only just met and the research role partner extending the invitation to the biochemistry colloquium is her academic advisor. But if the person offering the teaching workshop opportunity is an advanced biochemistry student who will be supervising the new student's work as a teaching assistant for the introductory biology course during her first semester, the doctoral student may experience some stress, not only about the immediate decision and her perceptions of the expectations held by each role partner but also because of the meaning her behavior holds for who she is. Her researcher and teacher identities would be in conflict. To favor one identity, she may need to adjust her self-perception of the other identity.

A less stressful scenario involving simultaneous activation of two identities with similar levels of salience and commitment will occur if the identities involve shared meanings. If the doctoral student's goals include conducting research on science learning and her advisor also values scholarly research on teaching, the student's identities will be consistent and mutually reinforcing (Burke, 2003b). Although she will still have to choose between activities because of the time conflict, she may be able to negotiate with her advisor and supervisor to determine which activity will the best for her integrated professional development.

Negative Impact of Multiple Identities. Too often, however, resolution of identity conflict is not as easy for future faculty—or, indeed, for current faculty—as portrayed in the example just given. Identities as teacher, researcher, participant in institutional governance, and provider of community service are all aspects of being a member of the academic profession. Much research about faculty work assumes that these identities and the activities associated with them are distinct, mutually exclusive, and conflicting (see Braxton, 1996; Colbeck, 1998). Similarly, colleges and universities evaluate faculty members' teaching, research, and service separately (Colbeck, 2002). This expectation that academic identities are distinct and separate has resulted in such problems as stress and reduced commitment to one or more roles.

Identity theory suggests that the current prioritization of research in doctoral programs and faculty careers may actually intensify feelings of time-related pressure and stress. According to Marks (1977), people tend to experience time and energy as scarce if the activities and role partners associated with their different identities are isolated from each other. This effect is exacerbated when people feel higher levels of commitment to some identities and lower levels of commitment to others. Thus doctoral students who are more highly committed to their researcher identities than teacher identities may resent time they must devote to teaching assistantships. This appears to be the case for many current faculty. Using data from nationwide surveys of U.S. faculty, Schuster and Finkelstein (2006) report that on average, faculty prefer to do research even as they face ever greater expectations to pay more attention to teaching, and the resulting stress may negatively affect their work.

One negative effect particularly relevant to doctoral education would occur if a student who has a high commitment to her identity as a teacher chooses not to subordinate it in order to make herself fit the dominant researcher identity promoted by the faculty in her program. In that case, a potentially excellent and well-rounded future faculty member might select herself out of the market for tenure-track positions in favor of fixed-term teaching-only positions, or she might leave the academy altogether. "When individuals are confronted with a persistent mismatch between identity meanings and perceptions of the social environment, one possibility is simply to exit the role" (Cast, 2003, p. 45n).

Benefits of Multiple Identities. Alternatively, theory and prior research about the positive effects of multiple identities in the work and family realm show how doctoral education can enable future faculty members to manage their several professional role identities successfully and productively (Colbeck, 2007; Marks, 1977; Thoits, 2003). Marks (1977), for example, theorized that individuals who feel high levels of commitment to each of several role identities may gain rather than lose energy as they engage in activities related to two or more of their identities. Furthermore, empirical research has found positive associations between active engagement in both work and family roles and mental well-being, physical health, self-esteem, and resilience in the face of setbacks (see Barnett and Hyde, 2001; Thoits, 2003).

Developing a sense of shared meanings across different identities, whether those identities are invoked within a single group or within intersecting groups (Burke, 2003b), may help doctoral students craft professional identities that integrate their identities as researcher, teacher, and service provider. Such integration may enhance their work efficiency and effectiveness.

Doctoral students' multiple identities may be activated concurrently within a single group. An example would be in a laboratory science research group led by the student's faculty advisor that employs undergraduates supervised by the doctoral student. In this example, the doctoral student's identities as advisee, researcher, and laboratory teacher may come to have similar levels of salience and commitment because they are activated together around the shared purpose of addressing a research problem. This role integration has the potential to reduce time-based conflicts while enhancing teaching effectiveness and scholarly productivity. In a recent qualitative study of role integration, faculty who perceived synergies among their academic roles found ways to accomplish multiple goals with single activities (Colbeck, 2007). One participant reported that his—and his doctoral students'—publication and grant productivity increased significantly after he added scholarly research about teaching in his discipline to his basic scientific research.

Doctoral students' multiple identities may also be activated simultaneously when they are in the presence of two groups of persons who do not usually overlap and who have differing sets of expectations for the student. An example of such a situation might involve a doctoral student with a pre-existing identity as a community activist. Because of her role as a respected leader of a community environmental group, she participates in a town-gown meeting involving other community members and university administrators in discussions about how the university might adopt sustainable practices that would initially involve some cost to the university but would enhance quality of life in the surrounding neighborhood. If the doctoral student brings her scholarly expertise to bear on helping the university and community group work toward agreement on a sustainability plan, the student's identities will reinforce each other (Burke, 2003b). Such role integration is likely to enhance her energy and productivity, especially if she documents and analyzes these efforts in publications that meet scholarly standards in her discipline (O'Meara, 2002).

Professional Work, Integrated Identities

Finding shared meanings and integrating all the professional identities involved in faculty work are important to enhance doctoral students' productivity, time and energy management, and well-being. But such an integrated understanding of faculty professional work is also important to the academy itself in order to slow the creeping deskilling and deprofessionalization of academic work (Rhoades, 1998). Professions are characterized by autonomy and professional authority, resting on expertise—distinctive bodies of knowledge that aspiring practitioners learn during long periods of specialized training. Professional work is complex and multilayered, and it involves expert judgment to solve nonroutine problems (Abbott, 1988; Scott, 2002). Hence a new faculty member educated to become an integrated professional is able to apply research skills to improve his teaching and his students' learning; to derive penetrating questions that advance his research agenda from thoughtful communication with students; and to define, analyze, and resolve real-world problems in partnership with interdisciplinary colleagues, students, and community members.

The notion that complicated and distinctive knowledge is embodied in well-educated professionals stands in stark contrast to another common way of managing complex work: bureaucratic division of labor (Scott, 2002). Abbott described the effect of dividing complex (and integrated) professional work into routine and nonroutine elements: "In every case, the eventual result has been the degradation of what had been professional work to nonprofessional status, sometimes accompanied by the degradation of those who do the work" (1988, pp. 125–126). He argues that division of labor between a "truly professional" group (such as tenured university professors) and a group with lower status and pay (such as fixed-term faculty with primary responsibility for teaching or directors of campus public service centers) undermines the lower-status group and places greater demands on the group who retain higher professional status. Such processes have occurred in medicine over the past few decades (Friedson, 2001) and are already at work in academe.

My concern here is less for the professional status of current and future faculty than for maintaining and enhancing the quality, creativity, effectiveness, and integrity of academic work. Fragmenting research, teaching, community engagement—not just into separate roles but into separate jobs—may enhance administrative flexibility and control, but at the expense of current and future faculty members' abilities to perceive and exploit connections. Such connections between research, teaching, and community service might enable them to address complex problems in ways that advance personal, economic, social, and public development. Educating doctoral students to find the synergistic connections between their multiple academic identities is a way of "reprofessionalizing" academic work, one student at a time.

Recommendations

Doctoral programs and their faculty should create contexts that encourage students to develop and integrate their professional identities of researcher, teacher, and engaged public scholar. According to Yehudi Elkana, president of the Central European University:

> Leaders in the disciplines must understand the critical roles of curricula and pedagogical work in their field and how deeply these functions are affected by the same epistemological understandings that relate to the research role. They must recognize, empirically, that most of those who earn the doctorate will spend far more time teaching and engaging with a variety of publics—in industry, policy, and community settings—than they will at the frontiers of science. Doctoral education must equip students to work in these settings [2006, p. 66].

Prior research has shown that current faculty integrate their research, teaching, and service more than they recognize. For some, the process of discussing their role and identity integration led them to realize how doing so has enhanced their work (Colbeck, 1998; 2007). If current faculty were encouraged to share the evolution and the effects of their professional identity integration with doctoral students, both groups would benefit. Specific classes, workshops, and programs can be designed or revamped to highlight benefits attainable from integrating research, teaching, and service identities.

Faculty and administrators can also foster integration of doctoral students' teaching, research, and service identities by creating cultures in their doctoral programs that elucidate shared meanings across the various aspects of academic work. For example, learning for the purpose of producing knowledge could be advocated as a mission that unifies teaching, research, and service (Lattuca and Colbeck, 2007). With that mission guiding all aspects of doctoral students' professional development, students might be more likely to perceive opportunities to integrate academic identities. For example, when a doctoral student is teaching undergraduates in the classroom, he may see his professional work as helping students develop deep understandings of knowledge they can use inside and outside the classroom. Similarly, the doctoral student may see his research as producing knowledge that can be used to advance theory or application in his discipline.

How doctoral students come to see themselves as professionals has implications far beyond the colleges and universities where they will become employed. These future faculty will become the educators and role models for future attorneys, nurses, business managers, industrial chemists, psychologists, journalists, and practitioners of many other professions who will learn their respective bodies of knowledge while attending degree programs in institutions of higher education. Universities, then, help define the professions (Brint, 1994), and "whatever model of professionalism prevails on campuses shapes the nature of professionalism in all professions" (Klay, Brower, and Williams, 2001, p. 46). Ideally, the students of faculty who are themselves integrated professionals will also learn how to accomplish complex work that requires judgment and skill (Friedson, 1994; Abbott, 1988) and to manage and integrate multiple professional and personal identities successfully.

References

Abbott, A. *The System of Professions: An Essay on the Division of Expert Labor.* Chicago: University of Chicago Press, 1988.

Austin, A. E., and McDaniels, M. "Using Doctoral Education to Prepare Faculty to Work Within Boyer's Four Domains of Scholarship." In J. M. Braxton (ed.), *Analyzing Faculty Work and Rewards: Using Boyer's Four Domains of Scholarship.* New Directions for Institutional Research, no. 129. San Francisco: Jossey Bass, 2006.

Barnett, R. C., and Hyde, J. S. "Women, Men, Work, and Family: An Expansionist Theory." *American Psychologist,* 2001, *56,* 781–796.

Braxton, J. M. (ed.). *Faculty Teaching and Research: Is There a Conflict?* New Directions for Teaching and Research, no. 90. San Francisco: Jossey-Bass, 1996.

Brint, S. *In an Age of Experts: The Changing Role of Professionals in Politics and Public Life.* Princeton, N.J.: Princeton University Press, 1994.

Burke, P. J. "Introduction." In P. J. Burke, T. J. Owens, R. T. Serpe, and P. A. Thoits (eds.), *Advances in Identity Theory and Research.* New York: Kluwer Academic/Plenum, 2003a.

Burke, P. J. "Relationships Among Multiple Identities." In P. J. Burke, T. J. Owens, R. T. Serpe, and P. A. Thoits (eds.), *Advances in Identity Theory and Research.* New York: Kluwer Academic/Plenum, 2003b.

Cast, A. D. "Identities and Behavior." In P. J. Burke, T. J. Owens, R. T. Serpe, and P. A. Thoits (eds.), *Advances in Identity Theory and Research*. New York: Kluwer Academic/Plenum, 2003.

Colbeck, C. L. "Merging in a Seamless Blend: How Faculty Integrate Teaching and Research." *Journal of Higher Education*, 1998, *69*, 647–671.

Colbeck, C. L. "Integration: Evaluating Faculty Work as a Whole." In C. L. Colbeck (ed.), *Evaluating Faculty Performance*. New Directions for Institutional Research, no. 114. San Francisco: Jossey-Bass, 2002.

Colbeck, C. L. "Academic Staff and Disciplinary Perspectives on Integrating Teaching and Research." Paper presented at the colloquium on International Policies and Practices for Academic Inquiry, Marwell, England, Apr. 2007.

Elkana, Y. "Unmasking Uncertainties, Embracing Contradictions: Graduate Education in the Sciences." In C. M. Golde and G. F. Walker (eds.), *Envisioning the Future of Doctoral Education: Preparing Stewards of the Discipline*. San Francisco: Jossey Bass, 2006.

Friedson, E. *Professionalism Reborn: Theory, Prophesy, and Policy*. Chicago: University of Chicago Press, 1994.

Friedson, E. *Professionalism: The Third Logic*. Chicago: University of Chicago Press, 2001.

Greenwood, E. "Attributes of a Profession." *Social Work*, 1957, *2*, 45–55.

Ibarra, H. "Provisional Selves: Experimenting with Image and Identity in Professional Adaptation." *Administrative Science Quarterly*, 1999, *44*, 764–791.

Klay, W. E., Brower, R., and Williams, B. "A Community-Oriented Model of Academic Professionalism." *Metropolitan Universities*, 2001, *12*(3), 14–50.

Lattuca, L. R., and Colbeck, C. L. "Producing Knowledge: An Integrated Public Research University Mission." In R. L. Geiger, C. L. Colbeck, R. L. Williams, and C. K. Anderson (eds.), *The Future of the American Public Research University*. Rotterdam, Netherlands: Sense Publishers, 2007.

Marks, S. R. "Multiple Roles and Role Strain: Some Notes on Human Energy, Time, and Commitment." *American Sociological Review*, 1977, *42*, 27–42.

O'Meara, K. "Uncovering the Values in Faculty Evaluation of Service as Scholarship." *Review of Higher Education*, 2002, *26*, 57–80.

Rhoades, G. *Managed Professionals: Unionized Faculty and Restructuring Academic Labor*. Albany: State University of New York Press, 1998.

Schuster, J. H., and Finkelstein, M. J. *The American Faculty: The Restructuring of Academic Work and Careers*. Baltimore: Johns Hopkins University Press, 2006.

Scott, W. R. *Organizations: Rational, Natural, and Open Systems*. Upper Saddle River, N.J.: Prentice Hall, 2002.

Silva, M. K. "Accreditation, Knowledge, and Strategies of Professionalizing Occupations." Unpublished doctoral dissertation, Department of Education Policy Studies, Pennsylvania State University, 2000.

Stryker, S. "Identity Salience and Role Performance." *Journal of Marriage and the Family*, 1968, *4*, 558–564.

Stryker, S., and Burke, P. J. "The Past, Present, and Future of an Identity Theory." *Social Psychology Quarterly*, 2000, *63*, 284–297.

Thoits, P. A. "Personal Agency in the Accumulation of Multiple Identities." In P. J. Burke, T. J. Owens, R. T. Serpe, and P. A. Thoits (eds.), *Advances in Identity Theory and Research*. New York: Kluwer Academic/Plenum, 2003.

CAROL L. COLBECK *is professor and dean of education at the University of Massachusetts Boston. Her research investigates how faculty integrate teaching, research, and service; how faculty teaching and organizational climate affect student learning; and how faculty balance professional and personal responsibilities.*

2

The pedagogies used in professional education to develop students' identities in the domains of knowledge, skills, and values can help doctoral programs better prepare future faculty members.

Applying Lessons from Professional Education to the Preparation of the Professoriate

Chris M. Golde

The concern that doctoral programs in the arts and sciences do not adequately prepare students for careers as faculty members is hardly a new one, but it has become urgent. Colleges and universities in United States are facing the impending retirement of large numbers of faculty members and need to replace them with qualified professionals, on or off the tenure track. The life of a faculty member—whether at a research university or a community college—requires balancing a number of roles and responsibilities in an evolving and stressful context. The preparation of graduate students for the modern professoriate must be rethought if the next generation of faculty members will be able to integrate their roles and serve as leaders of their disciplines and institutions.

In this chapter, I argue that the theoretical perspectives that are reshaping professional education may have considerable traction in helping rethink and recast traditional doctoral education. These ideas may be particularly fruitful in considering how future faculty should be prepared.

Rethinking Traditional Faculty Preparation

The traditional ways that have been used to prepare new faculty members are not particularly successful and deserve to be rethought. There is considerable evidence that new faculty members are not prepared for the professional life

New Directions for Teaching and Learning, no. 113, Spring 2008 © Wiley Periodicals, Inc.
Published online in Wiley InterScience (www.interscience.wiley.com) • DOI: 10.1002/tl.305

they enter (Gaff, 2002; Golde and Dore, 2001; Kennedy, 1997; Reis, 1997). Nor do postdoctoral positions provide explicit or adequate professional preparation (Davis, 2005). New faculty members are expected to arrive on campus ready to start work; there is little ramp-up time or on-the-job training.

What is the traditional preparation strategy? One pedagogical strategy might be dubbed the osmosis theory of learning. Doctoral students are expected to infer from years of observation how to be a faculty member. Although observation is a critical part of apprenticeship, many parts of faculty life are invisible to students. Indeed, faculty members rarely make the thinking and behind-the-scenes work of even the visible parts (like teaching) explicit. And without guidance and explanation, it is all too easy to draw the wrong conclusions solely from watching others work.

For other students, preparation for the professoriate is a matter of classical apprenticeship. A student who desires a faculty position finds a faculty member (often the primary advisor) to serve as mentor (or master, to use the language of apprenticeship) who will teach how to be an effective member of the profession. At its best, apprenticeship learning encompasses a range of roles—research, teaching, service, management, and advising—and a great deal of tacit knowledge about the ins and outs of the profession, including navigating departmental politics, networking in the discipline, integrating work roles, balancing work and personal life, and securing tenure. Often this relationship is neither formalized nor explicit, at least not in regard to the training the student receives as a prospective faculty member.

Unfortunately, the quality of such instruction varies enormously, in part because the mentors are neither taught to play that role nor rewarded for performing it well. There is no quality control, no assurance that information is current or correct. Nor can the student be confident of coverage of all aspects of professional practice. And because there is no system for matching masters and apprentices, access to this resource is haphazard. As a result, many students get little formal help, and others do not think to seek it out.

Other models may work better for educating future faculty. In fact, inspiration might be available from within the academy itself. I contend that the changes afoot in professional education to improve the preparation of future arts and sciences faculty members have promise. Given the disciplinary silos in the modern university, it is not surprising that those responsible for doctoral education in the arts and sciences are generally ignorant of the practices, debates, and innovative pedagogical strategies brewing among the faculty and administrators in professional schools.

In the category "professional education" I include the preparation of doctors, nurses, lawyers, the clergy, architects, and the like. A set of studies aimed at improving professional education was undertaken at the Carnegie Foundation for the Advancement of Teaching during my tenure at that institution. The Preparation for the Professions Program (PPP) is a series of two- to three-year comparative studies about the role of higher education in building professional understanding, skills, and integrity in law, engineering, medicine, nursing, and clergy. The PPP is led by Anne Colby and by William Sullivan, author of the influential book *Work and Integrity* (Sullivan, 2005). I am drawing extensively from the framing and findings of those projects for this chapter.

Lessons from Professional Education

The challenge for professional education is to prepare students for "the complex demands of professional work—to think, to perform, and to conduct themselves like professionals. The common problem of professional education is how to teach the complex ensemble of analytic thinking, skillful practice, and wise judgment upon which each profession rests" (Sullivan and others, 2007, p. 27). These, then, are three facets of professional life and professional expertise, each of which must be developed and integrated into a single professional identity. These three facets of expertise are, appropriately, three educational domains that students ought to encounter and participate in.

Building on recent advances in the learning sciences, the PPP studies refer to these three domains of professional education as the "three apprenticeships," opening the possibility of a wide variety of pedagogies, particularly observation and imitation. The *intellectual apprenticeship* emphasizes content knowledge and the ways of thinking inherent in the profession and discipline. Recall the character of Professor Kingsfield in the movie *The Paper Chase* and his repeated exhortations that students "think like a lawyer." The *skill apprenticeship* emphasizes doing. This is the domain of actually designing buildings, arguing cases, or performing surgery. To be sure, students typically begin with simple tasks, components of real-world complex practice, and advance step by step to more complicated activities. Novice tailors cut a lot of fabric and sew many seams before constructing an entire men's suit. Nursing students draw blood from mannequins and each other before doing so from patients.

The third apprenticeship, the *apprenticeship of identity and purpose,* introduces students to "the purposes and attitudes that are guided by the values for which the professional community is responsible. . . . The essential goal is to teach the skills and inclinations, along with the ethical standards, social roles, and responsibilities, that mark the professional" (Sullivan and others, 2007, p. 28). Many professions have codified ethical standards that seek to provide rules of conduct and an ethical touchstone of shared values. The medical field's Hippocratic Oath is one example.

Professional education evolved differently from doctoral education. Originally, professional practice was taught in classical apprenticeship style. Students entered into a formal relationship and engaged in several years of learning from a seasoned practitioner. Thereafter, they commenced practice on their own. During the late nineteenth and early twentieth centuries, the education of professionals moved into the university. "In broad terms this meant a movement away from apprenticeship (with its intimate pedagogy of modeling and coaching) toward reliance upon the methods of academic instruction (with its emphasis on classroom teaching and learning carried out far from the sites of professional practice)" (Sullivan, 2005, p. 195). This move offered advantages of uniformity of curriculum, easier enforcement of quality standards, and economies of scale essential as our society became more complex and ever more reliant on professionals.

The departments and schools that offer professional education in American research universities today incorporate elements of education by apprenticeship into their educational programs. Doctors get clinical training in teaching hospitals. Architecture students work in design studios where their work is subject to regular critique by faculty in front of peers. Theology students practice preaching and writing eulogies. Novice clinical psychologists meet with clients under supervision. Many law schools support community legal clinics. Educators employ a variety of pedagogical strategies that include simulations, role plays, approximations, projects, problem-based learning, practica, and internships. They incorporate feedback, coaching, self-reflection, and repetition into their teaching. The term *apprenticeship* reinforces the central importance of the pedagogies of participation and practice. These apprenticeship pedagogies are vital for learning skills and values and for applying theory and content to the contexts of professional work.

Not surprisingly, experts in teaching each of the three domains (and one of the critiques of professional education is that different groups of faculty cover the three apprenticeships) emphasize different pedagogies and rely on different forms of assessment. Of course, these pedagogical strategies are embedded in larger schooling-based structures, such as coursework, credit hours, and grades.

A body of knowledge is taught to each novice doctor or lawyer. The intellectual apprenticeship often relies on familiar classroom-based teaching and learning strategies. Imagine a medical student learning about disease processes, such as renal failure leading to death. She would read textbooks and attend lectures about the kidney, how it degenerates, what the stages of death are, and how to recognize them. She would demonstrate her mastery of the material through conventional classroom tests.

The second apprenticeship encompasses the body of skills shared by competent practitioners. These are often learned in practice, either in actual clinical settings with real clients or in simulated practice situations. Clinical education for doctors and nurses generally begins with observation, followed by simulations, and ultimately by trial-and-error learning on actual patients. When Pam Grossman and her colleagues (2005) studied education in three professions, they found that skillful teachers decompose complex practice, rendering the component parts visible to students and creating approximations so that students can repeatedly practice key activities before encountering actual clients.

Our same medical student would learn very different things about renal failure while working with simulated patients or attending actual patients in a teaching hospital. She would demonstrate competence by being able to diagnose kidney problems and treat them appropriately. Nevertheless, her skills training (with all the complicated and confusing ambiguities of an actual case) might seem quite disconnected and distant from her textbook knowledge.

The values or identity apprenticeship may also rely on observation and the pedagogies of practice. But while practice settings are probably crucial to learning values, self-reflection is also essential. Questions like "Why do I do it this way?" and "Could I do it differently?" are bound up with values, responsibility, and meaning. For our medical student, these are the moments of reflecting on why she wants to be a doctor and what kind of doctor she wants to be. How can she, for example, show empathy to the patient and family, especially when the patient is dying? How does she cope with her own feelings? Her mastery is her developing identity and confidence.

Ultimately the goal of professional education is to prepare professionals who integrate knowledge, skills, and values into one competent whole person. Sullivan says, "The essential goal is to teach the skills and traits, along with the ethical comportment, social roles, and responsibilities, that mark the professional. Through learning about and beginning to practice them, the novice is introduced to the meaning of an integrated practice of all dimensions of the profession, grounded in the profession's fundamental purposes" (2005, p. 208). Although far from perfect, medical education has made many strides in recent decades synthesizing theory, practice, and professional responsibility into relatively seamless educational models (Sullivan and others, 2007).

Pedagogies of Practice in Doctoral Education

The pedagogies of participation and practice are also well known—if not explicitly or deliberately incorporated—in doctoral education. Brown, Collins, and Duguid (1989) observed that the development of doctoral students as researchers often relies on these apprenticeship principles. Advanced graduate students "acquire their extremely refined research skills during the apprenticeships they serve with senior researchers. It is then that they, like all apprentices, must recognize and resolve the ill-defined problems that issue out of authentic activity, in contrast to the well-defined exercises that are typically given to them in textbooks and on exams throughout their earlier schooling. It is at this stage, in short, that students no longer behave as students, but as practitioners, and develop their conceptual understanding through social interaction and collaboration in the culture of domain, not of the school" (p. 40). Two hypothetical examples help illustrate how doctoral students learn to become historians or neuroscientists or mathematicians.

Doctoral programs in the sciences emphasize teaching and learning in the lab in the process of conducting research, rather than in the classroom. A first-year neuroscience doctoral student may take courses on neuroscience but will at the same time begin working in his advisor's research lab. He will start by conducting a discrete, well-defined research project assigned to him, learning the prevailing techniques of the lab from more advanced graduate

NEW DIRECTIONS FOR TEACHING AND LEARNING • DOI: 10.1002/tl

students and postdocs. Once he becomes technically competent and understands the science underlying the lab's research questions, he will work with the lab director to develop and execute a line of research that is consistent with the investigations funded and supported by the lab. Along the way he will contend with frustration when his experiments fail. He will present the results of his experiments, first to the lab group, then in a poster at a regional meeting, and ultimately in published papers. He will probably wrestle with ethical dilemmas—for example, what data to share and how much to withhold when making a presentation. He will have to square practical concerns with the norms and values of science.

Many humanities departments use parallel approaches for the development of students as teachers. A first-year graduate student in English might start by taking a class on how to teach freshman writing. This would be followed by a term in which she serves as a supervised teaching assistant (TA), taking a second course with fellow TAs, which provides an opportunity to discuss the challenges and problems that emerge from week to week. Her work leading discussion sections would be closely supervised by the faculty member running the lectures. Here she will be exposed to the complicated and unpredictable aspects of undergraduate classes, including syllabus preparation, book selection, classroom dynamics, developing discussions, disruptive or absent students, and the challenges of evaluation and grading. Over several years, she will have the opportunity to teach, reflect on her teaching, get feedback, and teach again. In subsequent years the student will take greater responsibility for supervising other students or teaching courses of her own devising.

The lens of the three apprenticeships is useful for examining the development of researchers or teachers. These two short hypothetical examples included the deliberate development of knowledge, skills, and values. Ideally, this happens for all doctoral students, whatever their discipline. Unfortunately, many students receive scant preparation as teachers and that even preparation as researchers may not involve the integration of all three apprenticeships.

Expanding our view to the preparation of new faculty members is not simply one of concatenating training for research with training in teaching. Of course, being a faculty member encompasses both teaching and research, but there is much more as well. What would the preparation of new faculty members based on the framework of the three apprenticeships look like? What are examples already in use?

The intellectual apprenticeship might robustly encompass direct preparation in research, teaching, and service. In addition, one might use workshops and "new faculty advice books" to introduce students to other faculty roles and responsibilities, how colleges and universities work, theories of teaching and learning, the demographic characteristics and lives of undergraduates, and the like. It is noteworthy that most efforts at formally preparing future faculty have taken the workshop and course approach. Traditional classroom-type pedagogy is the usual strategy.

Skill apprenticeship would build on the strategies used for developing researchers and teachers described earlier. In some programs, research training goes far beyond proposing and conducting one piece of research. Students have opportunities to practice the various steps of grant writing, submission, and revision. Likewise, some students have an opportunity to try all of the steps and stages of manuscript preparation, from an initial idea through publication. They could learn other aspects of faculty life by visiting other campuses and shadowing faculty. Some students learn to be advisors by supervising and mentoring undergraduates in the research lab. Other students learn about governance by participating in departmental hiring and curriculum committees.

I find it most difficult to find examples of ways to systematically tend to the third apprenticeship, inculcating the values that are part of the professoriate. Opportunities to explicitly discuss, observe, and enact the shared values of academic life are rare. Few students have or take the opportunity to reflect on why they are doing what they do and what kind of faculty member they want to be. When Jody Nyquist and her associates (1999) conducted longitudinal research with graduate students, they discovered how much students value opportunities to reflect and how rare such opportunities are. Relatedly, although universities are under pressure to provide graduate students with training in ethics and the responsible conduct of research, students often complain that the workshops amount to intellectually impoverished "how not to get caught" sessions with mandatory attendance. Clearly, opportunities are missed to help students develop professional judgment derived from a code of values and shared beliefs.

Final Questions

Being a faculty member at an American college or university in the twenty-first century involves complex and challenging work. It involves balancing a number of tasks and skills, each of which is enormously difficult and demanding. Moreover, faculty work is changing; it is becoming even more complicated, with expectations of doing more, more quickly, and with fewer resources and supports. If faculty members are valuable professionals in whose effective practice society has a great stake, then their complete (and integrated) professional education deserves considered attention.

This chapter offers a framework for understanding and rethinking the development and preparation of future faculty members that may have promise. The three apprenticeships—knowledge, skills, values—cover a wide landscape of identity development. The vision of an integrated professional life is one that will allow faculty members to move their fields, their institutions, and their students forward as this century progresses. Applying the framework and offering students opportunities to develop along all three dimensions will be challenging. And so I close this chapter with questions rather than answers.

New Directions for Teaching and Learning • DOI: 10.1002/tl

1. When and how can skill apprenticeship be built into the formal and informal curriculum? What useful approximations and simulations can be devised? Where are the opportunities for students to work in situations of authentic practice?
2. How can the values apprenticeship receive attention? What *are* the shared values and understandings of academe? How can they be modeled? When can students reflect on their emerging professional identities?
3. When, where, how, and under what circumstances should new educational experiences be incorporated into doctoral programs? Are programs already overloaded? Does ever-increasing time to degree coupled with student debt preclude meaningful reform?
4. For which students should such opportunities be available? All doctoral students? Or only those who are certain that they want to become faculty members?
5. The life of faculty members is quite different at different types of institutions. Is this as a unified profession? Or is preparation necessarily context-dependent?

It will require considerable effort and imagination to incorporate the pedagogies of participation and practice into traditional doctoral programs in order to prepare future faculty members more fully. Luckily, such pedagogies are already in use, at least in some doctoral programs, in the training of researchers and teachers. Models are available. We have foundations on which we can build.

Acknowledgments

I want to acknowledge the support and intellectual input from the Carnegie Initiative on the Doctorate team, George E. Walker, Andrea Conklin Bueschel, and Laura Jones. William Sullivan has been tremendously generous and encouraging, and his ideas have been enormously influential. Likewise, all of those involved with Carnegie's Preparing the Professions Program have helped develop my ideas.

References

Brown, J. S., Collins, A., and Duguid, P. "Situated Cognition and the Culture of Learning." *Educational Researcher,* 1989, *18,* 35–42.
Davis, G. "Doctors Without Orders: Highlights of the Sigma Xi Postdoc Survey." *American Scientist,* May-June 2005 (suppl.).
Gaff, J. G. "The Disconnect Between Graduate Education and Faculty Realities: A Review of Recent Research." *AAC&U Liberal Education,* 2002, *88*(3), 6–13.
Golde, C. M., and Dore, T. M. "At Cross Purposes: What the Experiences of Doctoral Students Reveal About Doctoral Education." Philadelphia: Pew Charitable Trusts, 2001. http://www.phd-survey.org/report.htm. Accessed Nov. 30, 2007.
Grossman, P., and others. "Unpacking Practice: The Teaching of Practice in the Preparation of Clergy, Teachers, and Clinical Psychologists." Paper presented at the

annual meeting of the American Educational Research Association, Montreal, Apr. 11–15, 2005.

Kennedy, D. *Academic Duty*. Cambridge, Mass.: Harvard University Press, 1997.

Nyquist, J. D., and others. "On the Road to Becoming a Professor: The Graduate Student Experience." *Change*, Mar. 1999, 18–27.

Reis, R. M. *Tomorrow's Professor: Preparing for Academic Careers in Science and Engineering*. New York: IEEE Press, 1997.

Sullivan, W. M. *Work and Integrity: The Crisis and Promise of Professionalism in America*. (2nd ed.) San Francisco: Jossey-Bass, 2005.

Sullivan, W. M., and others. *Educating Lawyers: Preparation for the Profession of Law*. San Francisco: Jossey-Bass, 2007.

CHRIS M. GOLDE is associate vice provost for graduate education at Stanford University. From 2001 through 2006, she served as research director for the Carnegie Initiative on the Doctorate and senior scholar at the Carnegie Foundation for the Advancement of Teaching.

3

Windows of opportunity for integrating community engagement throughout the doctoral career are offered in this chapter along with a description of the knowledge, skills, and value orientations needed for future faculty to become engaged scholars.

Graduate Education and Community Engagement

KerryAnn O'Meara

When graduate students are forming their ideas about research and scholarship and developing their professional identities, it is important that they take a broad view of scholarship. They must see the intellectual value of connecting ideas across academic disciplines, applying abstract ideas to real-world problems, and gaining theoretical insights from practice (Gaff, 2005).

Much has been written about preparing future faculty for involvement in multiple forms of scholarship and for multiple roles in various types of institutions (Austin, 2002; Austin and Barnes, 2005; Austin and McDaniels, 2006b; Pruitt-Logan and Gaff, 2004; Rice, 1996). Much has also been done to promote the development of graduate students as teachers such as the AACU's Preparing Future Faculty Program (Gaff, 2005). But there have been no national efforts to prepare and socialize early-career faculty for community engagement.

The lack of national attention to preparing future faculty for their roles as citizen-scholars represents a significant missed opportunity. Whereas graduate student involvement in engaged teaching and research, such as service-learning or community-based research, likely has immediate benefits for retention and learning, this chapter focuses on the impact of engagement during doctoral study on later community engagement when those doctoral students become faculty members. Graduate students who are not encouraged to see the relevance of their disciplines to local schools, governments, business, and the public are significantly less likely as faculty to

NEW DIRECTIONS FOR TEACHING AND LEARNING, no. 113, Spring 2008 © Wiley Periodicals, Inc.
Published online in Wiley InterScience (www.interscience.wiley.com) • DOI: 10.1002/tl.306

become engaged scholars (Tierney, 1997). Community engagement offers multiple avenues for integration of teaching, research, and outreach, an integration that many faculty yearn for but do not feel they have the skills to create (Bloomgarden and O'Meara, 2007; Colbeck, 1998). Therefore, understanding barriers to and facilitators of community engagement has implications for the institutionalization of community engagement in graduate programs, the quality of faculty work and satisfaction, and the fulfillment of college service missions.

Faculty who do not become involved in engagement cite such reasons as lack of fit between their discipline and engagement projects or disproportionate rewards for research and external funding rather than engagement (Abes, Jackson, and Jones, 2002; Colbeck and Michael, 2006). Further, in institutional environments focused on gaining prestige, it is difficult to create a reward system that sustains engagement (Colbeck and Michael, 2006; O'Meara, 2002; 2007). However, evidence from campus service-learning programs and research about service-learning across the disciplines (Colby, Ehrlich, Beaumont, and Stephens, 2003; Hollander and Hartley, 2000; Zlotkowski, 2000) show that faculty in all fields have designed careers that merge teaching, research, and service in ways that add to their disciplines, receive accolades, and enhance the education of their students. Lynton Award nominees (http://www.nerche.org) and Ehrlich Award winners (http://www.campuscompact.org) provide illustrations of the disciplinary diversity represented among faculty engaged in community work.

Certainly, concerns about prestige cultures, structural support, fit between faculty interests and community needs, and overloaded plates thwart faculty engagement. Reward systems in particular pose serious barriers to faculty engagement (Colbeck and Michael, 2006; O'Meara, 2002a, 2007; Ward, 2003). Reward systems, however, are made up in large part by faculty who are socialized in graduate school toward specific notions of what is and is not appropriate disciplinary scholarship.

The greatest barriers to future faculty community engagement may therefore be lack of imagination about how to connect disciplinary scholarship to public purposes; how to integrate teaching, research, and outreach toward meeting community needs; and how to fashion long-term careers as engaged scholars. What we need are the dispositions, orientations, investment, and commitment of professionals socialized toward engagement while in graduate school. This chapter interweaves literature and theory on graduate education with literature on engagement to envision how future faculty across disciplines might be prepared more intentionally to pursue engaged scholarship.

By "community engagement," I refer to work that engages faculty members' professional expertise to solve real-world problems in ways that fulfill institutional missions and are public, not proprietary (Driscoll and Lynton, 1999; Elman and Smock, 1985). This definition does not include work for which corporations or other organizations pay or if the results are privately owned. Like all scholarship, community engagement involves systematic inquiry, wherein the process and results are open to peer critique and disseminated (Hutchings and Shulman, 1999). The term *engagement* includes professional service and outreach, such as service-learning, community-based research, and applied research, that engage professional or academic expertise in partnership with local expertise to address real-world issues (Driscoll and Lynton, 1999). Engagement may involve teaching, research, or extension programs, and high-quality engagement will often be integrative, drawing on more than one type of faculty work. For example, research on exemplary engaged faculty shows that they have often developed long-term partnerships with community organizations involving service-learning opportunities for students and community-based research projects (O'Meara, 2006).

Graduate Education and Community Engagement: Why Now?

This is an ideal time to envision graduate education for engagement for several reasons. First, because significant numbers of faculty who began their careers in the 1960s and 1970s will be retiring (Austin, 2002), there is a special focus on preparing the generation of faculty who will begin their careers over the next five to ten years. Second, intense national attention on doctoral education through such projects such as the Responsive Ph.D. (Weisbuch, 2004), the Carnegie Initiative on the Doctorate (Golde and Walker, 2006; see also Chapter Two in this volume), and the Center for the Integration of Research, Teaching, and Learning (CIRTL) (see Chapter Six) demonstrate commitment among foundations, national associations, graduate deans, and researchers to improve graduate education so that it is more relevant to future careers and equitable for all groups (Austin and McDaniels, 2006a; Golde and Walker, 2006). Third, graduate students across disciplines have said that they want to be prepared for work that connects their intellectual passions with the needs of society but feel unprepared to do so (Austin and McDaniels, 2006a; Golde and Dore, 2001; Rice, Sorcinelli, and Austin, 2000). Fourth, many campus centers and undergraduate departments that have embedded service-learning in their programs for as long as two decades are poised to act as bridges to graduate student civic engagement. As Stanton and Wagner observe in their work on graduate education and civic engagement, "Many students experience the transition to graduate study as a withdrawal from public and community service that was a vital part of their undergraduate years" (2006, p. 2). Therefore, this is an ideal time to examine where to embed community engagement when socializing doctoral students for faculty careers.

Graduate Education and Socialization Theory

During the process of socialization, a person takes on characteristics, values, and attitudes, as well as knowledge and skills, that contribute to a new professional self (Austin and McDaniels, 2006a). Socialization theory posits that graduate education influences how students understand their work, what work is considered important and desirable, and how one goes about it as a professional. Because graduate education occurs mainly within disciplinary departments, effective socialization for community engagement must be embedded within the courses, programs of study, and dissertation experience of specific departments and disciplines (Austin and McDaniels, 2006b).

Weidman, Twale, and Stein (2001) apply Thornton and Nardi's framework for role acquisition (1975) to the socialization of graduate and professional students. In doing so, Weidman, Twale, and Stein (2001) identify four overlapping stages of graduate student development: the *anticipatory stage,* the *formal stage,* the *informal stage,* and the *personal stage.* During these stages, three core elements of socialization—*knowledge acquisition, investment,* and *involvement*—lead to identification with and commitment to a professional role (Thornton and Nardi, 1975). Austin and McDaniels (2006a) suggest that throughout the stages and elements of socialization, doctoral students should be intentionally mentored toward specific sets of knowledge, skills, and professional attitudes and habits and the cultivation of professional networks.

This chapter focuses on specific knowledge, understandings, skills, professional orientations, and values that future faculty might acquire during preparation to become engaged scholars. Different phases of a doctoral career suggest "windows of opportunity" where critical experiences may foster their interest in and commitment to engagement. Clearly, graduate education differs considerably for doctoral students in philosophy, computer science, or education. However, all doctoral students acquire professional and academic skill sets as they are inducted into their professional or disciplinary communities. Furthermore, because engagement involves teaching through service-learning or community-based research (or both), graduate students who learn to become engaged scholars simultaneously learn to become integrated professionals who connect different aspects of their work.

A Doctoral Program in Four Phases

Community engagement can be incorporated into doctoral study at various points. I use Weidman, Twale, and Stein's four stages of socialization, three core elements of socialization, and related theory and research on the socialization process (see Table 3.1) to organize incorporation of engagement. Aspects of each of the Weidman, Twale, and Stein stages and core elements, as well as critical experiences described, may occur throughout all four phases, however, and the time it takes to complete doctoral programs and the ways in which students advance from novice to expert vary widely. While many experiences, both structured and informal, will be discussed in this section, there is no substitute for engaged faculty scholars who intentionally open doors to engaged ways of knowing, learning, teaching, and discovering and show their protégés how to open such doors themselves.

NEW DIRECTIONS FOR TEACHING AND LEARNING • DOI: 10.1002/tl

Phase One: Orientation: Marketing Programs and Recruiting Students. Prospective students want to see their passions and interests represented at the institutions they wish to attend. For example, when selecting an undergraduate institution, I attended a college tour. There a senior described helping build a library and classrooms for an orphanage in Tijuana, Mexico, as part of a college project. Almost immediately, my choice was made, as I could see myself beside community members, students, and faculty engaged in this work. This college attracted students with similar interests to participate in significant service-learning and community partnerships. Similarly, socializing graduate students for roles as engaged scholars begins with who and how programs recruit. Programs can communicate to thousands of prospective students who engaged in service-learning as undergraduates about opportunities to continue such work during doctoral study. Marketing materials and informational sessions can highlight assistantships with service-learning or community-based research projects and include quotes from students, faculty, and community partners who are engaged in university-community partnerships. By creating intentional bridges for engaged undergraduate majors, prospective graduate students will know that doctoral education in their chosen fields will involve them in work that they believe is worthwhile.

Research suggests that early personal and professional experiences with engagement influence faculty adoption of this type of scholarship and that women and faculty of color self-report more involvement in community engagement than their white male counterparts (Colbeck and Michael, 2006). Many prospective graduate students will be women and people of color, two groups who have experienced problems establishing themselves during the initial period of graduate work, in part because they often find two activities that attracted them to graduate school, teaching and service, less valued than research (Aguirre, 2000; Antonio, Astin, and Cress, 2000; Tierney and Bensimon, 1996). Therefore, establishing a pipeline for engagement involves assertively recruiting women, students of color, and students who have shown prior interest in this work.

During the *anticipatory stage* of graduate education, students have preconceived notions of what it means to be a doctoral student and a professor, gathered from the media, undergraduate experiences, and other interactions (Weidman, Twale, and Stein, 2001). As new students interact with current students and faculty, they learn about program requirements and attempt to understand what this new life will be like. They observe faculty and advanced students to "learn what is valued, what work is done, and what the role of a faculty member involves" (Austin and McDaniels, 2006a, p. 12). New students find peers with whom to associate, find a faculty mentor, and seek financial support (Braxton and Baird, 2001). Each of these activities could be linked more intentionally with community engagement.

Introductory seminars could present students with multiple options for scholarship. Traditional research paradigms and methods and basic and

Table 3.1. Embedding Community Engagement in the Socialization and Preparation of Future Faculty

Time Period	Related Socialization Concepts	Understandings and Skills	Critical Experiences
Orientation to the program: recruitment and first six months	Anticipatory stage	Understanding engagement as a way of learning and teaching within a discipline.	Recruiting students who have been involved in engagement; showcasing the work Connecting engaged faculty mentors and student protégés Securing community engagement related graduate assistant positions
Taking core courses: first three years	Formal stage and knowledge acquisition	Understanding of history of engagement in the discipline Skills in designing and facilitating high-quality service-learning Skills in framing research questions toward public purposes Learning research methods appropriate for engaged work in the discipline Skills in communicating results to multiple venues Appreciation for ethical behavior and a sense of responsiveness to community partners Interpersonal skills in dialogue, teamwork, and collaboration.	Embedding engagement in coursework Exposure to philosophical background of experiential education and social theories of education Experience as a teaching assistant for a course where service-learning is integrated Courses, concentration, and certificate programs in participatory action research Course assignments such as mock grant proposals, news releases, newsletter accounts, grant reporting, and presentations before boards Opportunities to work with community partners on grant projects, designing the questions and activities collaboratively

Developing mastery (finishing coursework, taking comprehensive exams, working on dissertation)	Informal stage and involvement	Institutional savvy and management skills Understanding of reward systems and how colleges work Entrepreneurial spirit and ability to garner resources Finding, creating, and participating in professional communities within and outside academe Integrative skills	Role modeling and personal conversations Serving on university committees on outreach Exposure to human resource challenges of managing a staff, practice developing budgets, grant-writing, and advocating for projects to campus and to external stakeholders Invitations to co-present at disciplinary and engagement conferences, introduction to other engaged scholars
Making commitments (last six to twelve months, finishing dissertation, job searching, and beginning new faculty role)	Personal stage and investment	Understanding how engagement fits into the student's life as a scholar	Active participation in professional communities Sharing one's dissertation with other engaged scholars Making connections between personal, political, and social commitments and engagement Assistance by faculty mentor in researching different institutional types and the implications for engaged work Mentorship in finding a faculty position and in orientation to early career

purely theoretical work will remain staples of graduate education in every discipline. However, presentation of alternative forms of scholarship (such as public history projects wherein students and faculty collect and analyze oral histories and archival documents to help communities preserve their history) will show doctoral students that multiple forms of scholarship in their fields are legitimate, rigorous, and desirable. Many future scholars may decide that community engagement does not fit their teaching or research interests. Later, however, when sitting on a promotion and tenure committee for someone who does community engagement, prior exposure may make them more appreciative of its contributions.

Moreover, doctoral students have the opportunity to "reframe" the group they are considering or have joined (Tierney and Rhoads, 1994). Simply by asking questions about community engagement during initial interviews, bringing engaged interests and skills to assistantships, and challenging established ways of knowing and priorities for the field, graduate students can encourage their new departments to become more open to engagement.

Phase Two: Taking Core Courses. In discussing in this section the knowledge, understandings, and skills learned throughout the first three years of graduate study, I build on the work of Austin and McDaniels (2006a, 2006b) and the Carnegie Initiative on the Doctorate (Golde and Walker, 2006). Whereas each provides holistic pictures of doctoral student development, I focus here on understandings and skills necessary for development of engaged scholars.

Understandings and Skills. During the coursework phase, most graduate students attempt to gain foundational and specialized knowledge. During this period, which overlaps with the *formal stage* of Weidman, Twale, and Stein (2001), students "receive formal instruction in the knowledge upon which future professional authority will be based" (p. 13), and they engage in *knowledge acquisition* that shifts from general to more specialized and complex knowledge. Students learn normative role expectations and "interpret their environment, establish their professional goals, and seek positive feedback and modification in their continued growth and development" (p. 13). By assuming roles as teaching or research assistants, by learning about exemplary scholars, and by learning the history and accomplishments of their disciplines, doctoral students begin to form professional identities.

Not only must engagement scholars gain a generic history of scholarship in their discipline (Austin and McDaniels, 2006a, 2006b), but they must also learn about the intellectual history and "heroes" of applied work. Formally, in courses and seminars, faculty might highlight as role models the work of engaged scholars at their own institutions or those for whom national disciplinary service awards are named (such as the Solon T. Kimball Award for Public and Applied Anthropology or the Margaret Mead Award given by the American Anthropological Association). Doctoral students can learn how their disciplines have benefited from the theoretical and practical contributions of these scholars. Informally, faculty mentors can

NEW DIRECTIONS FOR TEACHING AND LEARNING • DOI: 10.1002/tl

share their own understanding of contributions from community engagement to their discipline. Doctoral students can serve on selection committees for community engagement awards. Doctoral students should also learn their institution's history of community engagement, including mistakes, such as exploitation of community members.

Doctoral students should also be exposed early to engaged teaching skills, such as constructing syllabi, setting learning goals for classes (Austin and Barnes, 2005), merging learning goals with community partner needs, and embedding service opportunities in curricular planning. As teaching assistants, graduate students can prepare undergraduates for service experiences, fostering awareness of differences in social capital between community and university partners. Reflection about how students' identities (in terms of race and ethnicity, income, education, and language) compare to those of their community partners will help all be more successful in embracing and transcending similarities and differences. Deep conversations about pedagogy should include consideration of philosophies behind experiential education (such as those of Kolb, 1984, and Dewey, 1916), which posit that the most effective learning takes place when reflection and action are combined. Eyler and Giles's work on the "learning behind service-learning" (1999) describes the qualities of "high-quality placements" and "well-integrated experiences" that engage students in meaningful service experiences with community members. Such reflection will help budding engaged scholars create assignments that help undergraduates make analytical connections between course material and service-learning experiences (Eyler and Giles, 1999; Strand and others, 2003). Faculty mentors might collaborate with doctoral students on classroom research to assess undergraduate outcomes of service-learning, from personal development to disciplinary learning (Strand and others, 2003), and submit findings for presentation or publication.

In doctoral study, students learn criteria for excellence in their discipline, including how scholars ask questions and pursue answers (Austin, 2002). Engaged scholars should also develop understandings and skills in research methods appropriate to engaged work in their discipline, including strategies and ethics related to participatory action and community-based research (Austin and Barnes, 2005; Austin and McDaniels, 2006b). For example, compared to traditional research, community-based research tends to involve more collaboration between academic researchers and community members, makes use of multiple methods of discovery and dissemination, and has social change as an explicit goal (Strand and others, 2003). For some disciplines, community-based research methods are not very different from the research methods for other work; challenges arise in framing research questions and projects in ways that have immediate application to real-world problems. Faculty might provide opportunities for doctoral students to practice such skills in classroom assignments and grant applications.

Research on assessment of engaged work as scholarship suggests that faculty who have successful careers in engagement produce multiple products from each engaged project, such as a peer-reviewed journal article, a presentation, a community organization report, products related to pedagogy, and press releases (O'Meara, 2002). It is critical both for faculty careers and for enhancing the visibility of engaged work that future faculty communicate results clearly and in a variety of ways to reach multiple audiences. Programs can have doctoral students practice such skills by preparing their final class projects as mock grant proposals, news releases, newsletter accounts, or journal articles. In addition, students can communicate project results to community partners and help partners disseminate information about projects to grant agencies and trustees of nonprofits.

Researchers are often guests in communities that are not their own. Future faculty should develop appreciation for ethical behavior and a sense of responsiveness to community partners. They should be prepared to consider ethical issues related to all forms of scholarship (Austin, 2002; Austin and McDaniels, 2006a; 2006b). In preparation for engaged scholarship, doctoral students should particularly reflect on issues of differential power and privilege between university actors and those with whom they work. The learning might include discussions about sharing resources, sharing credit for outcomes, and building community capacity through partnerships.

When faculty engage in successful campus community partnerships, they develop mutual trust and respect, communicate clearly and listen carefully, understand and empathize with each other, remain flexible, and share power (Strand and others, 2003). Because engaged work depends on trust and communication among diverse partners, graduate students should have opportunities to develop their interpersonal skills (Austin and Barnes, 2005), especially in dialogue, teamwork, and collaboration (Austin and McDaniels, 2006a). As the dean of a college of education said in one case study of an engaged campus, "It takes a special set of skills to work in the community, and not everyone [in a given faculty] has them" (O'Meara, 2002b, p. 125). This may mean listening to community partners' ideas for projects that have nothing to do with one's discipline, teaching, or scholarly interests and helping establish relationships with their colleagues.

Structured and informal suggestions for fostering development of these skills and understandings include modeling, personal conversations, professional seminars, internships, and certificates to develop knowledge and skills for multiple forms of scholarship, opportunities to concentrate in community-based research, and support for community-based master's and doctoral theses (Austin and McDaniels, 2006a; Strand and others, 2003). Doctoral students learn first and foremost about academic work, however, through observation of faculty (Austin, 2002). There are many opportunities for faculty to make informal impressions in the hallway, in the lab, or while traveling to a research site.

Professional Orientations and Values. As doctoral students work with engaged professors, their *involvement* will engender a *professional orientation* that encourages connecting knowledge with real-world problems. During the "middle period" of doctoral study, students most often identify their intellectual and professional interests and commit to a particular set of research questions and methods (Braxton and Baird, 2001). Students should be exposed to community-based research projects during coursework and have opportunities to shape these activities in their own departments.

Doctoral students should consider for themselves why they should become involved in community engagement. According to Strand and colleagues (2003), although there are clear benefits for institutions, students, disciplines, and faculty from involvement in community-based research, the answer to this question should emphasize democracy and helping community-based organizations access and use resources to enhance capacity for community development. Some graduate students' answer to this question may be based on how they think about knowledge or their epistemology. Colbeck and Michael (2006) observe that faculty who practice engaged work often display a solidarity approach to knowing, a concept developed by McAfee (2000) in her research on political ways of knowing, wherein knowledge is pursued through examination of contexts such as history, customs, experiences, and values. Likewise, engaged students and faculty may answer the question because of how they view the role of their discipline in the world.

Phase Three: Developing Mastery (Taking Exams, Working on the Dissertation). As students prepare for comprehensive exams, develop dissertation proposals, and engage in dissertation research, they continue to develop understandings, skills, and a professional orientation.

Understandings and Skills. Although doctoral students may not develop *institutional savvy and managerial skills* within the first years of graduate study, they could be developing such skills by their third or fourth year. These include developing a political understanding of how the institution and community partner organizations work, reaching out to other campus units, and making engagement programs visible on campus (Singleton, Burack, and Hirsch, 1997). Case study research on successful enclaves of public service in colleges and universities found that "the success of service-enclaves depends on how skillfully the people in them read their institutional cultures and locate points of convergence between their goals and the goals of the institution" (Singleton, Burack, and Hirsch, 1997, p. 22). Similarly, Walshok (1995) found that the most successful campus outreach programs enjoyed intellectual and political support of campus leadership.

Also, funded and institutionalized engagement projects often employ undergraduates and professional staff in the university and in the community, and faculty often supervise these staff. So doctoral students need exposure to the challenges of staff management (Austin and McDaniels, 2006a) that might come from being a staff member, developing organizational charts and plans for implementation of projects, collecting materials for fieldwork, supervising student staff, and helping with the logistics of transportation and publicity. Doctoral students should have opportunities to manage communication among stakeholders, including ensuring that funding agencies, community partners, institutional allies, staff, and students are all informed of engagement activities.

Knowledge of *how reward systems work* in departments and universities will help doctoral students understand that values such as "scholarship consists of discovering theoretical knowledge that sets the scholar apart from others" and "true scholarship can be found in top-tier journals" can work against positive evaluations of their engaged work (O'Meara, 2002). Therefore, doctoral students should learn to *document the scholarly aspects* of their engagement (Driscoll and Lynton, 1999). They also develop a professional network of senior and midcareer scholars who will understand their work and be able to support their tenure or contract renewals.

Doctoral students might develop an *entrepreneurial spirit* and the *ability to garner resources* for engaged work (Singleton, Burack, and Hirsch, 1997) through practice in grant-writing, building and managing budgets for engagement projects, searching out new opportunities for collaborative projects, and gathering various stakeholders together to design projects. Faculty mentors can involve doctoral students in the financial aspects of engaged work to help them understand the staff positions and community projects that may be in jeopardy if support cannot be found for programs. Likewise, faculty mentors can explain how they align their projects with institutional priorities and opportunities and provide guidance about granting agencies and foundation relationships to cultivate as early professionals.

Future engaged scholars should be exposed to faculty mentors who model and talk about their integration of teaching, research, and engagement. Through this exposure, doctoral students may develop *integrative skills,* which involve perceiving and establishing linkages between teaching, research, and outreach (Colbeck, 1998). Faculty who can integrate their engagement with their other faculty roles are likely to experience numerous benefits, including improved teaching and research (Colbeck, 1998; Bloomgarden and O'Meara, 2007). Faculty role models who integrate their work make these connections visible to students and are able to discuss benefits and challenges of integration.

Finding and participating in *professional communities* related to engaged work will provide additional sources of practical and moral support. Austin and McDaniels (2006a) and Vicki Sweitzer (Chapter Four in this volume) discuss the importance of nurturing professional networks, including junior colleagues, contemporaries, and more senior peers from other institutions. Nationally, networks and journals have developed around engaged work, such as the annual conference on Teacher Education and Service-Learning in Engineering, and graduate students should be introduced to them.

Professional Orientation and Values. During the *informal stage,* students learn role expectations through interactions with others (Weidman, Twale, and Stein, 2001). As students move through the middle and final parts of their doctoral programs, they begin to feel more comfortable in their environments. They know the language and have begun to develop specialized expertise. Students are embedded in a peer culture that shares information, provides support, and celebrates rites of passage (Austin and McDaniels, 2006a; Weidman, Twale, and Stein, 2001). At this stage, students are in an ideal position to reflect on the values and beliefs that guide scholarly work in their disciplines. Table 3.2 provides a description of values and beliefs that seem to guide engaged scholarship across disciplines. These values and beliefs are often learned through faculty role-modeling, conversations with students, and conversations with community partners.

Phase Four: Making Commitments: Completing the Dissertation and Becoming Faculty. In the final, personal stage of socialization discussed by Weidman, Twale, and Stein (2001), "individuals and social roles, personalities and social structures become fused" (Thornton and Nardi, 1975, p. 880). Students make decisions about whether to invest their time, self-esteem, social status, and reputation further in pursuit of faculty careers. Weidman, Twale, and Stein (2001, p. 36) observe that "the outcome of socialization is not the transfer of a social role, but identification with and commitment to a role that has been normatively and individually defined." During this final stage, faculty can reinforce doctoral students' professional identities as engaged scholars by nominating them for awards related to community engagement, by sharing positive recommendations of their engaged dissertation work, and by introducing them to colleagues with similar values at conferences.

Table 3.2. Values Guiding Engaged Scholarship

Values and Beliefs Regarding the Process of Scholarship

- Engaged scholars value the process used to make knowledge.
- Engaged scholars want the process to be as transformative, democratic, and inclusive as possible.
- Engaged scholars try to share power and space, knowledge, and resources with community partners.

Values and Beliefs Regarding the Products of Scholarship

- Engaged scholars value disseminating the products of their work in the places where it will have the most impact.
- Engaged scholars give credit to community partners for collaborative work.

Values and Beliefs Regarding the Location of Scholarship

- Engaged scholars are attentive to their own locations in higher education institutions and the social capital and resources therein.
- Engaged scholars respect indigenous knowledge in communities and have a heightened sensitivity to cultural literacy and relevance.

Sources: Strand and others, 2003; O'Meara, 2002a, 2002b

Faculty mentors can play a significant role as prospective engaged scholars search for academic positions. Because some methods used in engaged scholarship, including participatory action research, are not considered mainstream for dissertations in many fields, faculty advocates can help in preparing applications and by placing phone calls to colleagues to facilitate placement. Also, faculty should encourage students to consider the range of institutional missions when applying for faculty jobs (Austin and McDaniels, 2006b) because the mission, norms, and reward system of an institution will very much influence faculty capacity to be involved in engaged work (Colbeck and Michael, 2006). Thus faculty mentors should help their student protégés find institutional environments likely to provide organizational support to enhance their chances for success.

Conclusion

Several assumptions underlie the strategies for embedding community engagement in graduate education outlined in this chapter. One assumption is that there are concrete ways to connect graduate study to societal needs. A second is that doing so revitalizes graduate education while contributing significantly to society. A third assumption is that isolating doctoral programs from society limits the creativity, sense of responsibility, knowledge and skill development of future scholars. A fourth assumption is that the knowledge, skills, and values that graduate students acquire while becoming engaged scholars will also help them grow as professionals who find satisfaction in integrating different kinds of faculty work.

Tierney (1997) recommends that organizations use socialization processes as opportunities to re-create rather than simply replicate their cultures. In that spirit, this chapter suggests that graduate education needs to be "disrupted," "re-created," and "renewed" to include community engagement as an attractive way of learning, knowing, and doing within disciplines. Transforming who is recruited to graduate school and how students learn while there means infusing the academy and disciplines with new values regarding the process, products, and locations of scholarly work. Embedding engagement in graduate education will attract students who are eager to envision careers that open doors between universities, disciplines, and the world.

References

Abes, E., Jackson, G., and Jones, S. "Factors That Motivate and Deter Faculty Use of Service-Learning." *Michigan Journal of Community Service Learning*, 2002, 9, 5–17.

Aguirre, A. *Women and Minority Faculty in the Academic Workplace*. ASHE-ERIC Higher Education Report 27, no. 6. San Francisco: Jossey-Bass, 2000.

Antonio, A. L., Astin, H. S., and Cress, C. M. "Community Service in Higher Education: A Look at the Nation's Faculty." *Review of Higher Education*, 2000, 23, 373–398.

Austin, A. E. "Preparing the Next Generation of Faculty: Graduate School as Socialization to the Academic Career." *Journal of Higher Education*, 2002, 73, 94–122.

Austin, A., and Barnes, B. "Preparing Doctoral Students for Faculty Careers That Contribute to the Public Good." In A. Kezar, T. Chambers, J. Burkhardt, and Associates. *Higher Education for the Public Good: Emerging Voices from a National Movement*. San Francisco: Jossey-Bass, 2005.

Austin, A. E., and McDaniels, M. "Preparing the Professoriate of the Future: Graduate Student Socialization for Faculty Roles." In J. C. Smart (ed.), *Higher Education: Handbook of Theory and Research*, Vol. 21. New York: Springer, 2006a.

Austin, A. E., and McDaniels, M. "Using Doctoral Education to Prepare Faculty to Work Within Boyer's Four Domains of Scholarship." In J. M. Braxton (ed.), *Delving Further into Boyer's Perspectives on Scholarship*. New Directions for Institutional Research, no. 129. San Francisco: Jossey-Bass, 2006b.

Bloomgarden, A., and O'Meara, K. "Faculty Role Integration and Community Engagement: Harmony or Cacophony?" *Michigan Journal of Community Service Learning*, 2007, *13*(2), 5–18.

Braxton, J. M., and Baird, L. L. "Preparation for Professional Self-Regulation." *Science and Engineering Ethics*, 2001, *7*, 593–610.

Colbeck, C. L. "Merging in a Seamless Blend: How Faculty Integrate Teaching and Research." *Journal of Higher Education*, 1998, *69*, 647–671.

Colbeck, C. L., and Michael, P. "Individual and Organizational Influences on Faculty Members' Engagement in Public Scholarship." In R. A. Eberly and J. R. Cohen (eds.), *Public Scholarship*. New Directions for Teaching and Learning, no. 105. San Francisco: Jossey-Bass, 2006.

Colby, A., Ehrlich, T., Beaumont, E., and Stephens, J. *Educating Citizens: Preparing Americas Undergraduates for Lives of Moral and Civic Responsibility*. San Francisco: Jossey-Bass, 2003.

Dewey, J. *Democracy and Education*. New York: Macmillan, 1916.

Driscoll, A., and Lynton, E. (eds.). *Making Outreach Visible: A Workbook on Documenting Professional Service and Outreach*. Washington, D.C.: American Association for Higher Education, 1999.

Elman, S. E., and Smock, S. M. *Professional Service and Faculty Rewards: Toward an Integrated Structure*. Washington, D.C.: National Association of State Universities and Land-Grant Colleges, 1985.

Eyler, J., and Giles, D. E. *Where's the Learning in Service-Learning?* San Francisco: Jossey-Bass, 1999.

Gaff, J. G. "Preparing Future Faculty and Multiple Forms of Scholarship." In K. O'Meara and R. E. Rice (eds.), *Faculty Priorities Reconsidered: Rewarding Multiple Forms of Scholarship*. San Francisco, Jossey-Bass, 2005.

Golde, C. M., and Dore, T. M. *At Cross Purposes: What the Experiences of Doctoral Students Reveal About Doctoral Education*. Philadelphia: Pew Charitable Trusts, 2001. http://www.phd-survey.org/report.htm. Accessed Nov. 30, 2007.

Golde, C. M., and Walker, G. E. (eds.). *Envisioning the Future of Doctoral Education: Preparing Stewards of the Discipline*. San Francisco: Jossey-Bass, 2006.

Hollander, E., and Hartley, M. "Civic Renewal in Higher Education: The State of the Movement and the Need for a Natural Network." In T. Ehrlich (ed.), *Higher Education and Civic Responsibility*. Phoenix: Oryx Press, 2000.

Hutchings, P., and Shulman, L. S. "The Scholarship of Teaching: New Elaborations, New Developments." *Change*, May 1999, pp. 11–15.

Kolb, D. *Experiential Learning: Experience as a Source of Learning and Development*. Upper Saddle River, N.J.: Prentice Hall, 1984.

McAfee, N. *Habermas, Kristeva, and Citizenship*. Ithaca, N.Y.: Cornell University Press, 2000.

O'Meara, K. "Uncovering the Values in Faculty Evaluation of Service as Scholarship." *Review of Higher Education*, 2002a, *26*, 57–80.

O'Meara, K. "Scholarship Unbound." In Phillip Altbach (series ed.), *Studies in Higher Education Dissertation Series*. New York: RoutledgeFalmer, 2002b.

O'Meara, K. "Faculty Motivation for Engagement: Listening to Exemplars." Paper presented at the Association for the Study of Higher Education community meeting, Anaheim, Calif., Nov. 4, 2006.

O'Meara, K. "Striving for What? Exploring the Pursuit of Prestige." In J. C. Smart (ed.), *Higher Education: Handbook of Theory and Research,* Vol. 22. New York: Springer, 2007.

Pruitt-Logan, A. S., and Gaff, J. G. "Preparing Future Faculty: Changing the Culture of Doctoral Education." In D. H. Wulff, A. E. Austin, and Associates, *Paths to the Professoriate: Strategies for Enriching the Preparation of Future Faculty.* San Francisco: Jossey-Bass, 2004.

Rice, R. E. *Making a Place for the New American Scholar.* New Pathways Inquiry, no. 1. Washington, D.C.: American Association for Higher Education, 1996.

Rice, R. E., Sorcinelli, M. D., and Austin, A. E. *Heeding New Voices: Academic Careers for a New Generation.* New Pathways Working Papers, no. 7. Washington, D.C.: American Association for Higher Education, 2000.

Singleton, S., Burack, C., and Hirsch, D. "Organizational Structures for Community Engagement." Working Paper no. 21. Boston: New England Resource Center for Higher Education, 1997.

Stanton, T. K., and Wagner, J. W. "Educating for Democratic Citizenship: Renewing the Civic Mission of Graduate and Professional Education at Research Universities." 2006. http://la.ucla.edu/Events/CCL%20grad%20conference/position%20paper.pdf. Accessed Nov. 30, 2007.

Strand, K., and others. *Community-Based Research and Higher Education: Principles and Practices.* San Francisco: Jossey-Bass, 2003.

Thornton, R., and Nardi, P. M. "The Dynamics of Role Acquisition." *American Journal of Sociology,* 1975, 80, 870–885.

Tierney, W. G. "Organizational Socialization in Higher Education." *Journal of Higher Education,* 1997, 68, 1–16.

Tierney, W. G., and Bensimon, E. M. *Promotion and Tenure: Community and Socialization in Academe.* Albany: State University of New York Press, 1996.

Tierney, W. G., and Rhoads, R. A. *Enhancing Promotion, Tenure and Beyond: Faculty Socialization as a Cultural Process.* ASHE-ERIC Higher Education Report, no. 6. Washington, D.C.: George Washington University, School of Education and Human Development, 1994.

Walshok, M. L. *Knowledge Without Boundaries: What American Research Universities Can Do for the Economy, the Workplace, and the Community.* San Francisco: Jossey-Bass, 1995.

Ward, K. *Faculty Service Roles and the Scholarship of Engagement.* ASHE-ERIC Higher Education Report, no. 29. San Francisco: Jossey-Bass, 2003.

Weidman, J. C., Twale, D. J., and Stein, E. L. *Socialization of Graduate and Professional Students in Higher Education: A Perilous Passage?* ASHE-ERIC Higher Education Report, no. 28. Washington, D.C.: George Washington University, School of Education and Human Development, 2001.

Weisbuch, R. "Toward a Responsive Ph.D.: New Partnerships, Paradigms, Practices, and People." In D. H. Wulff, A. E. Austin, and Associates, *Paths to the Professorate: Strategies for Enriching the Preparation of Future Faculty.* San Francisco: Jossey-Bass, 2004.

Zlotkowski, E. "Service-Learning in the Disciplines." *Michigan Journal of Community Service Learning,* 2000, 61–67 (special issue).

KERRYANN O'MEARA *is associate professor of higher education at the University of Maryland at College Park. Her research focuses on the ways in which we socialize, reward, and support the growth of faculty so that they can make distinct contributions to the goals of higher education.*

Bringing together mentoring, social networks, and professional identity theories, this chapter explores how messages received from network partners influenced the professional identity development of business doctoral students in their first semester of study.

Networking to Develop a Professional Identity: A Look at the First-Semester Experience of Doctoral Students in Business

Vicki L. Sweitzer

The academic career is becoming increasingly more competitive and is shaped primarily by what is rewarded, especially what will earn tenure, at both the institutional and disciplinary levels. This trend is becoming the norm at most types of institutions but is most prevalent at research-oriented institutions. Because of these pressures, performance expectations become overwhelming and may result in "careerism." Huber (2002) defines careerism as worrying less about the quality and more about the rate and number of publications and waiting until after tenure to pursue areas of personal interest, such as teaching or slower-producing lines of research. Even in professional institutions such as business schools, the quantity of refereed publications is becoming the predominant currency for career advancement. Acceptance rates in top-tier journals are decreasing, however, and there are fewer openings each year for tenure track positions at top-rated institutions.

Faculty and administrators involved in doctoral education, including business, are responding to these pressures by training students to succeed based on what is rewarded by peers. An unintended by-product may be the development of a fragmented conception of the faculty career (Colbeck,

NEW DIRECTIONS FOR TEACHING AND LEARNING, no. 113, Spring 2008 © Wiley Periodicals, Inc.
Published online in Wiley InterScience (www.interscience.wiley.com) • DOI: 10.1002/tl.307

1998; 2002). Fragmentation occurs when research, teaching, and service are viewed as mutually exclusive and in opposition to each other (Colbeck, 2002). In addition, these doctoral programs are not preparing students for jobs off the tenure track at institutions other than research universities. According to Schuster and Finkelstein (2006), nearly 35 percent of faculty are appointed off the tenure track on term contracts. Such contracts are becoming the norm at four-year and two-year institutions. Research institutions are also increasing their use of contingent staffing options (Schuster and Finklestein, 2006).

Higher education scholars such as Austin and Wulff (2004) argue that graduate education in general is suffering from a fragmented view of academic work, and the upcoming generation of faculty is ill-prepared for careers both in and outside of the academy. To combat this fragmentation, national programs such as Preparing Future Faculty and Alliances for Graduate Education in the Professoriate are encouraging graduate programs to emphasize multiple aspects of doctoral education. One notable example is the heightened focus on the teaching assistant role as critical to an integrated conception of the faculty career (Wulff, Austin, Nyquist, and Sprague, 2004).

Changes in the conception of doctoral education require shifts in the ways researchers investigate doctoral education and the doctoral student experience. New studies should account for the messages students receive about integration or fragmentation of roles from a variety of people. For example, researchers have suggested that students' peer relationships play an important role in doctoral student development (Tinto, 1993; Weidman, Twale, and Stein, 2001), yet few studies examine the variety of relationships that students form while pursing a doctoral degree and how those relationships influence their professional identity development.

In this chapter, I describe a study that provides a theoretical lens for examining the doctoral student experience that accounts for the multiple relationships that facilitate or stifle doctoral student development. One important outcome of students' relationships is the development of a professional identity as integrated scholar or fragmented professional.

Prior research that examined the student-advisor dyad has certainly contributed to our current understanding of the doctoral student experience and time to degree (Golde, 2000; Green and Bauer, 1995). However, these studies often fail to acknowledge that doctoral students' relationships with others outside their academic programs are likely to contribute to their development as early as the first semester. According to Chris Golde (Smallwood, 2004), attrition is consistent across the three stages of doctoral education, with approximately a third leaving at each stage (the first year, predissertation, and dissertation stage). Student experiences in the earliest stage are likely to have a strong influence on personal development and persistence in year two and beyond. Therefore, this study addressed the following questions:

- Which relationships appear to be most influential during the first semester of the doctoral student experience?

NEW DIRECTIONS FOR TEACHING AND LEARNING • DOI: 10.1002/tl

- How (if at all) do these relationships begin to affect the development of an integrated or fragmented professional identity?

Bringing together mentoring, social networks, and professional identity theories, this study used case study methodology to explore how positive and negative support received from network partners influenced the professional identity development process for business doctoral students. Becker and Carper (1956) noted that identification with an occupation occurs as early as the first year of study. This study captured information about the messages communicated and received between doctoral students and their networks of advisors, peers, friends, and family members to understand how doctoral students begin to see themselves as integrated scholars or fragmented professionals.

Theoretical Framework

Mentoring and social networks theories provide theoretical lenses for examining the doctoral student experience. Doctoral students are likely to have relationships with many types of individuals, including peers, faculty, friends, family, and business associates, who may provide various types of support, friendship, advice, or developmental assistance throughout a student's doctoral program. Social networks research examines different types of networks (friendship, advice, developmental), often independently of each other, whereas mentoring research frequently focuses on a dyadic relationship. This study draws on mentoring, social networks, and professional identity theories to examine *which* network members provide *what types* of support, *how* they provide that support, and *to what extent* that support influences the development of an integrated or fragmented professional identity during the first semester of doctoral study.

Mentoring Theory. Research on mentoring has provided insight into the role relationships play on individual development in career, social, and organizational contexts. A mentoring relationship exists when a more experienced organizational member provides a less experienced organizational member with support, thereby enabling the less experienced individual to navigate the socialization process and career progression. However, mentoring relationships have also been found to occur among peers and via computer (Kram and Isabella, 1985; Bierema and Merriam, 2002). Mentoring studies have found that such relationships can enhance career outcomes such as promotion, raises, and job satisfaction (Arnold and Johnson, 1997; Whitely, Dougherty, and Dreher, 1991) and offer psychosocial benefits that may include role-modeling, development of competencies, and work-role effectiveness (Kram, 1985). Another still underresearched outcome of mentoring relationships is the assistance mentors provide in helping protégés find their calling or professional identity (Kram, 1985; Levinson and others, 1978).

New Directions for Teaching and Learning • DOI: 10.1002/tl

More than two decades ago, Kram (1985) proposed the relationship constellation, suggesting that a variety of relationships with peers, supervisors, friends, family, and subordinates may provide a range of developmental functions, including support for the development of a professional identity. As careers become increasingly competitive, one mentor may no longer be sufficient. In fact, recent mentoring research has found that individuals are connecting with a diverse array of mentors because one individual alone may lack the time, skills, or expertise needed to provide adequate support (de Janasz, Sullivan, and Whiting, 2003). Individuals with multiple mentors experience more career benefits than individuals with a single mentor (Higgins, 2000; Higgins and Thomas, 2001; Seibert, Kraimer, and Liden, 2001; Van Emmerick, 2004). It is therefore reasonable to assume that doctoral students also rely on many individuals, not just a single academic advisor, for support. This study consequently examines the relationships doctoral students bring with them and develop as early as the first semester to elucidate how those relationships help them navigate the doctoral student experience and contribute to the development of an integrated or fragmented professional identity.

Social Networks Theory. Whereas mentoring research focuses on the outcomes of relationships between individuals, social networks theory provides a framework for examining the *interactions* that occur in those relationships. Social networks theory seeks to explain how a network of actors establish and maintain connections in an organizational context and how those connections facilitate a multitude of outcomes, such as professional advancement, information acquisition, and identity development (Ibarra, 1999; Ibarra, Kilduff, and Tsai, 2005; Kadushin, 2004). Network analysts examine structural properties of networks, rather than individual attributes such as gender or ethnicity, in order to understand behavior beyond that of dyadic relationships. "They concentrate on studying how the pattern of ties in a network provides significant opportunities and constraints because it affects the access of people and institutions to such resources as information, wealth, and power" (Wellman, 1983, p. 157).

Using social networks theory as a theoretical lens for examining doctoral student development allows for critical examination of an individual's access to organizational and career-related information and resources through interactions with others. Lack of information and resources or exposure solely to redundant information may be one reason why doctoral students develop a fragmented conception of the faculty career. The messages students receive from their various network partners are likely to influence their perceptions of the various academic roles (research, teaching, and service) and allocation of time to these roles. These messages, in turn, are likely to influence doctoral students' professional identity development process.

Developmental Networks: The Marriage of Mentoring and Social Network Theories. In 2001, Higgins and Kram proposed the "developmental network," the "set of people a protégé names as taking an active interest in and action to advance the protégé's career by providing developmental assistance" (p. 268). Similar to theories of mentoring, the developmental network perspective suggests that assistance may include career and psychosocial support. The concept of developmental networks brings together mentoring and social networks theories to offer a holistic view of the doctoral student experience, examining the nature of a student's relationships with multiple others as critical to preparation as a future faculty member. One outcome of the support received by an individual from members within his or her social network is the development of a professional identity (Ibarra, Kilduff, and Tsai, 2005).

Professional Identity. Professional identity is defined as "the perception of oneself as a professional and as a particular type of professional" (Bucher and Stelling, 1977, p. 213). Professional identity is relatively stable and encompasses the attributes, beliefs, values, motives, and experiences that help individuals define themselves in a professional role (Schein, 1978). Individuals present certain personas that convey the qualities prescribed by their profession, such as competence, judgment, and trustworthiness, with the hopes that others will ascribe those same qualities to them (Ibarra, 1999). Some of these qualities may already be basic elements of one's identity, but others may be incongruent, and some may be developed through experience.

In *The Elements of Identification with an Occupation*, Becker and Carper (1956) studied the professional identities of graduate students in physiology, philosophy, and mechanical engineering. They found that the more the graduate students identified concretely with these four major elements of work (occupational title, commitment to task, commitment to particular organizations, and significance for one's position in the larger society), the more difficult it was for them to consider changing professions or associating with an organization that did not offer opportunities for their chosen profession.

Recent research has explored the *process* by which one develops a professional identity. For example, Ibarra's work on provisional selves (1999) noted that individuals early in their career must convey a credible image, yet they have not fully internalized that professional identity. Thus identities crafted in the early career stages are only provisional and must be revised and developed through experience. Dobrow and Higgins (2005) examined the influence of developmental relationships on the clarity of one's professional identity. Using a three-wave longitudinal design, they asked full-time M.B.A. students about their multiple relationships and clarity of professional identity. They found that as developmental network density increased and students had less access to nonredundant resources, the clarity of their professional identity decreased. Similar issues may be at work for doctoral students and will likely offer insight into how they develop professional identities as fragmented (focused on only one role) or integrated (perceiving connections across multiple roles).

Methods

This exploratory study aimed to reveal how twelve first-semester doctoral students in five business disciplines (accounting, finance, marketing, management and organization, and supply chain) begin to develop professional identities as future faculty members as they interacted with network partners. A network partner is an individual, either inside or outside of the academic community, with whom a student forms a relationship. The study was conducted at a top-rated research institution, referred to as Valley University, with a top-fifty-ranked business program. Because one goal of the study was to build new theory about the process by which doctoral students develop professional identities, Valley University's College of Business was chosen as an "extreme case" due to its strategic mission to focus on research, socialization of Ph.D. students as primarily researchers, and goal to place Ph.D. graduates in other highly ranked colleges of business. Extreme cases assist with theory building (Eisenhardt, 1989; Pratt, Rockmann, and Kaufmann, 2006). Data collection included semistructured interviews with doctoral students supplemented with direct observations and interviews with student-identified network partners and other faculty members at the Valley University College of Business.

Interviews. To obtain information about the doctoral student experience and the professional identity development process, I interviewed all first-year business Ph.D. students ($n = 12$), their identified network partners ($n = 19$), and other faculty and administrators most involved with doctoral students during the first semester ($n = 5$). Students were interviewed the first week of the fall 2005 semester and the first week of the spring 2006 semester. Student interview questions elicited information about the qualities perceived as necessary for success in a doctoral program, the most influential relationships (network partners) to date, expectations of network partners, how expectations were communicated, and what it means to be a doctoral student, research assistant, and teacher. Network partner interviews elicited information regarding overall program expectations, how expectations are communicated, the types of support provided to help students achieve expectations, and student abilities needed to be successful.

Observations. At the beginning of the fall 2005 semester, all first-year Ph.D. students were required to attend a one-day collegewide orientation. During orientation, I conducted semistructured observations focusing on the messages communicated to the first-year students by faculty, administrators, and advanced students. I focused on how they defined and conveyed expectations for the roles of doctoral student, research assistant, and teacher. I also collected information about program and disciplinary requirements for the first year of study and beyond.

At the start of the spring 2006 semester, all students (except those with prior college-level teaching experience) were required to attend a one-and-one-half-day teaching camp. My observations focused on the messages communicated about balancing research and teaching, undergraduate student advising, and how to develop successful undergraduate courses.

Analyses and Findings

I followed guidelines outlined by Miles and Huberman (1994) and Yin (2003) to conduct within-case and cross-case analyses to capture information about each student's first-semester experience. I will now discuss findings regarding (1) the messages students received, (2) the sources of the messages, (3) the influence of those messages on the students' development of integrated or fragmented professional identities, and (4) meaningfulness versus reward.

The Messages Students Receive. The doctoral students took away four major messages from orientation: "publish or perish" ($n = 5$), "research is king" ($n = 4$), "must place in the top fifty" ($n = 3$), and "high expectations" ($n = 3$). During interviews, students expressed apprehension, primarily because most were inexperienced and lacked understanding about how to conduct research. Some students felt immediate pressure to start the research process, which caused further anxiety. One student noted, "You are going to have to publish, publish, publish. And you need to have at least six [publications] by the time that you finish." Other students left orientation realizing that research was the only acceptable and recognized contribution at the Valley University College of Business.

Students said less about teaching camp. Several students noted that learning about the resources available and hearing the experiences of faculty from multiple disciplines was helpful. One faculty member in particular shared his love and interest in teaching as his initial reason for pursuing a Ph.D. and entering academia. A student pushed the faculty member on this point by saying, "I thought we weren't supposed to want to teach; the program wants us to focus on research." The faculty member responded, "I meant to tell you to keep that interest personal, at least while you are here." Several students discussed this interaction during interviews, admitting that teaching was also one of the reasons they were pursuing a Ph.D. But they had learned from conversations with advanced students and messages conveyed at orientation that expressing their teaching interests was not advisable at this early stage of the doctoral program.

To put students' comments in context, I interviewed individuals they had identified as important network partners, including advanced students and faculty in the academic community, along with family, friends, and business associates outside of the program. The information shared by network partners within the Valley University College of Business community was consistent with what the first-year students described. One third-year student noted, "I feel as if the message comes across that [teaching] is not the goal, and we certainly shouldn't admit that that is what you want to do in the beginning." A fifth-year student discussed program expectations: "They don't want you to be too good at teaching, but you've got to be good enough. If you are too good, that is a bad signal. If you are really bad, that is a bad signal because they can't sell you. So you need to be within some range of decent—a little above average, but not exemplary."

I also interviewed faculty advisors and Ph.D. coordinators from each of the five disciplines. All described the doctoral program as rigorous and aimed at training students to become researchers. All said teaching was a part of the doctoral student experience but not the priority at the student or faculty levels, nor did faculty spend much time helping doctoral students learn to be effective in the classroom. One faculty advisor acknowledged that teaching was important but noted that "teaching would not be a constant agenda item for discussion."

Messages students received from network partners outside the academic community about program performance and placement were less focused on research. When I asked a student's spouse about the importance of placement and publication, the spouse noted, "I think he can have publications while in school. I think he can get a reasonably good placement and sell himself. It is more a question of if he wants to really invest all his efforts in this, so I tell him to pick a school he will be happy with." Another spouse said his only expectations were that his wife "gain confidence and be the strong, intelligent woman that I know she is and decide what she wants postgraduation because she loves teaching and helping others."

Students' Networks: Sources of the Messages. Because this study uses social networks as a theoretical foundation, the relationships that students came with or were developing would likely inform how they begin to develop professional identities as future faculty members. Previous research discusses the faculty advisor as the most important relationship for doctoral students (Baird, 1990; Golde, 2000; Green, 1991). Only six of the twelve doctoral students in this study, however, discussed their faculty advisor as having an important influence on their first-semester experience. Most mentoring studies focus solely on mentors within a protégé's organizational context as influential for career progression (Aryee, Wyatt, and Stone, 1996; Ragins and Cotton, 1999). Indeed, in this study, seven of the twelve students identified only relationships with other members of their academic community as important to their first-semester progress. Five students identified their influential network partners as individuals both within and outside of the academic community. Thus relationships outside a protégé's organization, including family, can provide valuable support and be influential for career progression.

Influence of Messages on Professional Identity Development: Integration Versus Fragmentation. Doctoral students' reflections about what it means to be a researcher focused on three areas. First, students viewed the research assistant role as an opportunity to build research skills. Second, their discussions of the role were limited to tasks because they still lacked research experience. Finally, students viewed research as less of an un-known. Few of the twelve students had prior research experience, so they learned about research by observing faculty and advanced students, partic-ipating in research projects, and reading research papers. A few students mentioned that being a research assistant is geared toward "developing prac-tical skills" and "learning what to do with data." Most of the students spoke of general research tasks, such as collecting data, analyzing data, and con-ducting literature reviews. This exposure to tasks provided first-year stu-dents with some sense of the research process. One student noted, "I'm excited about the research, and I feel much more comfortable that it's some-thing that I can do. I have to improve and get better at it, but . . . it's not so much of an unknown." None of the students discussed the outcomes of research, however, or expressed an understanding of why one would con-duct research, such as finding practical or theoretical contributions that influence practice. It appeared that for some students, initial experiences increased their confidence as researchers, thereby strengthening this part of their identity.

The doctoral students described the teacher role in two ways. First, students again focused on tasks, but now the tasks of teaching. Second, stu-dents viewed teaching as an obligation or a distraction from research. Many of the first-year students had limited teaching experience, so they relied on conversations with faculty or advanced students to ascertain what teaching meant at a research-oriented institution. Most students described the impor-tant tasks of teaching as being prepared for class, working through class problems, and solid presentation. Other students described teaching as "being the first line of defense" and "playing mediator and dealing with crowd control." In addition to describing the teaching tasks, five students viewed teaching as an obligation or distraction from their primary task of conducting research. For example, one student stated that teaching is a "duty and not something to be enthusiastic about." Another student noted, "Here at [Valley], . . . it seems like teaching is a necessary evil. . . . We went out with one of the younger professors, and he was telling me, 'It's a pain I have to teach this semester, blah, blah, blah.'" None of the doctoral students mentioned learning or student development as outcomes of teaching or as important responsibilities of instructors.

When comparing doctoral students' perceptions of research and teach-ing, I found that those who identified network partners within and outside of the academic community had less critical perceptions of teaching than students who identified network partners solely within the Valley Univer-sity business school community. Students with a combination of network partners internal and external to the academic community were still ques-tioning the notion that research is more important, and they were unsure if top-fifty placement was right for them. For example, one student identi-fied only one network partner outside the academic community, and he described teaching as a "beautiful thing" and "a way to increase knowledge." A student whose network included doctoral cohort and family members described teaching as "personally important" and "an opportunity to help others." Another student who relied on faculty and family support said he was still undecided about his primary focus. He believed that once he figured out which was more important personally, research or teaching, he would know if attending Valley University was the correct decision. Thus students' networks and the messages communicated by their network partners seemed to influence the degree to which they saw teaching and research in competition with each other or as complementary.

Meaningfulness Versus Reward. I asked faculty during interviews to reflect on what it meant to be a faculty member at a top-fifty business program. Specifically, I asked what aspects of their work were most meaningful to them and what aspects were most rewarded at the disciplinary and institutional levels. Their responses shed light on what they conveyed to doctoral students and the challenges faculty members themselves faced. While several faculty discussed research as personally meaningful and the most likely (or only) activity that would garner extrinsic rewards, many also regarded teaching, building relationships, collaborations among colleagues and institutions, writing book chapters, and influencing organizational practice as intrinsically rewarding. In fact, several faculty mentioned the satisfaction they felt when they learned that their research had influenced practice. Yet these same faculty also acknowledged that most practitioners do not read the academic journals in which faculty must publish for consideration for promotion and tenure.

A Ph.D. coordinator described how doctoral students are trained as teachers: "In terms of teaching, we expect that you [students] perform at a high level, but you shouldn't be spending a lot of time on that, if you will." He further commented that not much time, from the faculty perspective, is spent on training students to be teachers. However, later in the interview, I asked him to tell me what work was most personally meaningful. He said, "It's kind of weird how there is synergy between teaching and research, and teaching a Ph.D. seminar makes me better as a researcher. And so being at an institution that has a strong doctoral program makes me better as a researcher, even though [teaching] sucks up some of my time in terms of taking it away from my research." His comments highlighted the challenges of managing research and teaching apparent at the faculty level as well as for the doctoral students participating in this study.

Discussion

This study offered a new theoretical lens for examining the doctoral student experience and provided evidence that many students rely on multiple individuals for support beyond their academic advisors or peers. The students' personal relationships served as sources of support and offered insights into program and institutional expectations. The empirical evidence that developmental networks influence professional identity development, even in early career stages, is consistent with Dobrow and Higgins's findings (2005). However, this study offers a different perspective on the issue of network density than that offered by the Dobrow and Higgins study. The findings from this study suggest that students who relied solely on network partners from within the academic community, and therefore had more access to redundant information, were more likely to have a fragmented view of the faculty career after one semester. This result, however, likely stems from the strong Valley University College of Business's emphasis on research over teaching for both faculty and doctoral students. This study therefore also offers insight into the challenges faculty face in preparing doctoral students for multiple and overlapping roles as professors. The question is, on what basis should students be trained: what is rewarded, what is personally meaningful, or what is of value to society? Or might it be possible to accommodate all three? Regardless of the answer, the Valley University College of Business experience indicates that doctoral students are confronting the conflicts and fragmentation between teaching and research that exists in top doctoral programs.

Researchers such as Austin and Wulff (2004) have suggested that the graduate student experience is the first phase of socialization into the faculty career, and other research has shown that the most important phase of professional identity development occurs in the early-career years (Ibarra, 1999; Schein, 1978). Therefore, the messages that students receive in the early stages of doctoral education are likely to set the tone for future socialization efforts and to influence student perceptions of what it means to be a faculty member. Identifying what messages are communicated about academic careers, understanding who communicates those messages, and determining how, if at all, doctoral students internalize the messages are crucial to understanding how future faculty are (and should be) prepared. The students who prioritized relationships both within and outside the Valley University College of Business were still questioning the message that research is more important than teaching and were not convinced that a top-fifty institution was where they wanted to be upon completion of their Ph.D. programs. By the end of the first semester, these students still perceived some linkages between teaching and research. Conversely, the students who relied solely on individuals within the Valley University academic community, with its strong research bias, were more inclined to accept program and institutional expectations for research. For these students, research and teaching identities were fragmented. Thus the context and the network may influence professional identity development. The more dependent students were on relationships with network partners solely within the academic community, the more their professional identities resembled those advocated by that academic community.

Implications

The message that research is of utmost importance is not inconsistent with Valley University's institutional mission. Valley University students were being trained for careers at top-fifty business programs, and the faculty were providing a "realistic job preview" as early as possible in the doctoral student experience. There may be two unintended outcomes. First, students were developing a fragmented conception of the faculty career. Second, the students who do not place at top-fifty research institutions upon completion of their doctorates may be ill-prepared for the teaching and advising loads they are likely to encounter. Several faculty noted that teaching is becoming more important for initial placement, even at research institutions. Yet the faculty at Valley University acknowledged that they did not provide adequate training for students beyond research skills. Valley University's challenge is likely shared by other doctoral programs: to decide between training students based solely on program or institutional mission or developing students in all areas of faculty life to ensure adequate preparation for multifaceted academic careers.

References

Arnold, J., and Johnson, K. "Mentoring in Early Career." *Human Resource Management Journal,* 1997, 7(4), 61.

Aryee, S., Wyatt, T., and Stone, R. "Early Career Outcomes of Graduate Employees: The Effect of Mentoring and Ingratiation." *Journal of Management Studies,* 1996, 33, 95–118.

Austin, A. E., and Wulff, D. H. "The Challenge to Prepare the Next Generation of Faculty." In D. H. Wulff, A. E. Austin, and Associates, *Paths to the Professoriate: Strategies for Enriching the Preparation of Future Faculty.* San Francisco: Jossey-Bass, 2004.

Baird, L. L. "The Melancholy of Anatomy: The Personal and Professional Development of Graduate and Professional School Students." In J. C. Smart (ed.), *Higher Education: Handbook of Theory and Research,* 1990, 6, 361–392.

Becker, H. S., and Carper, J. "The Elements of Identification with an Occupation." *American Sociological Review,* 1956, 21, 341–347.

Bierema, L. L., and Merriam, S. B. "E-Mentoring: Using Computer-Mediated Communication to Enhance the Mentoring Process." *Innovative Higher Education,* 2002, 26, 211–227.

Bucher, R., and Stelling, J. G. *Becoming Professional.* London: Sage, 1977.

Colbeck, C. L. "Merging in a Seamless Blend: How Faculty Integrate Teaching and Research." *Journal of Higher Education,* 1998, 69, 647–671.

Colbeck, C. L. "Integration: Evaluating Faculty Work as a Whole." In C. L. Colbeck (ed.), *Evaluating Faculty Performance.* New Directions for Institutional Research, no. 114. San Francisco: Jossey-Bass, 2002.

de Janasz, S. C., Sullivan, S. E., and Whiting, V. "Mentor Networks and Career Success: Lessons for Turbulent Times." *Academy of Management Executive,* 2003, 17, 78–91.

Dobrow, S. R., and Higgins, M. C. "Developmental Networks and Professional Identity: A Longitudinal Study." *Career Development International,* 2005, 10, 567–583.

Eisenhardt, K. M. "Building Theories from Case Study Research." *Academy of Management Review,* 1989, 4, 532–550.

Golde, C. M. "Should I Stay or Should I Go? Student Descriptions of the Doctoral Attrition Process." *Review of Higher Education,* 2000, 23, 199–227.

Green, S. G. "Professional Entry and the Adviser Relationship." *Group and Organization Studies,* 1991, *16,* 387–407.

Green, S. G., and Bauer, T. N. "Supervisory Mentoring by Advisors: Relationships with Doctoral Student Potential, Productivity, and Commitment." *Personnel Psychology,* 1995, *48,* 537–562.

Higgins, M. C. "The More, the Merrier? Multiple Developmental Relationships and Work Satisfaction." *Journal of Management Development,* 2000, *19,* 277–296.

Higgins, M. C., and Kram, K. "Reconceptualizing Mentoring at Work: A Developmental Network Perspective." *Academy of Management Review,* 2001, *26,* 264–288.

Higgins, M. C., and Thomas, D. A. "Constellation and Careers: Toward Understanding the Effects of Multiple Developmental Relationships." *Journal of Organizational Behavior,* 2001, *22,* 223–247.

Huber, M. T. "Faculty Evaluation and the Development of Academic Careers." In C. L. Colbeck (ed.), *Evaluating Faculty Performance.* New Directions for Institutional Research, no. 114. San Francisco: Jossey-Bass, 2002.

Ibarra, H. "Provisional Selves: Experimenting with Image and Identity in Professional Adaptation." *Administrative Science Quarterly,* 1999, *44,* 764–791.

Ibarra, H., Kilduff, M., and Tsai, W. "Zooming In and Out: Connecting Individuals and Collectivities at the Frontiers of Organizational Network Research." *Organization Science,* 2005, *16,* 359–371.

Kadushin, C. "Introduction to Social Network Theory," 2004. http://home.earthlink.net/~ckadushin/Texts/Basic%20Network%20Concepts.pdf. Accessed Nov. 30, 2007.

Kram, K. E. *Mentoring at Work: Developmental Relationships in Organizational Life.* Glenview, Ill.: Scott, Foresman, 1985.

Kram, K. E, and Isabella, L. A. "Mentoring Alternatives: The Role of Peer Relationships in Career Development." *Academy of Management Journal,* 1985, *28,* 110–132.

Levinson, D. J., Darrow, C. N., Klein, E. B., Levinson, M. A., and McKee, B. *Seasons of a Man's Life.* New York: Knopf, 1978.

Miles, M. B., and Huberman, A. M. *Qualitative Data Analysis: An Expanded Sourcebook.* (2nd ed.) Thousand Oaks, Calif.: Sage, 1994.

Pratt, M. G., Rockman, K. W., and Kaufmann, J. B. "Constructing Professional Identity: The Role of Work and Identity Learning Cycles in the Customization of Identity Among Medical Residents." *Academy of Management Journal,* 2006, 235–262.

Ragins, B. R., and Cotton, J. L. "Mentor Functions and Outcomes: A Comparison of Men and Women in Formal and Informal Mentoring Relationships." *Journal of Applied Psychology,* 1999, *84,* 529–550.

Schein, E. H. *Career Dynamics: Matching Individual and Organizational Needs.* Boston: Addison-Wesley, 1978.

Schuster, J. H., and Finkelstein, M. J. "On the Brink: Assessing the Status of the American Faculty." *Thought and Action,* Fall 2006, pp. 51–62.

Seibert, S. E., Kraimer, M. L., and Liden, R. C. "A Social Capital Theory of Career Success." *Academy of Management Journal,* 2001, *44,* 219–237.

Smallwood, S. "Doctor Dropout." *Chronicle of Higher Education,* Jan. 16, 2004, p. A10.

Tinto, V. *Leaving College: Rethinking the Causes and Cures of Student Attrition.* Chicago: University of Chicago Press, 1993.

Van Emmerick, I.J.H. "The More You Get the Better: Mentoring Constellations and Intrinsic Career Success." *Career Development International,* 2004, *9,* 578–594.

Weidman, J. C., Twale, D. J., and Stein, E. L. *Socialization of Graduate and Professional Students in Higher Education: A Perilous Passage.* ASHE-ERIC Higher Education Report, no. 28. Washington, D.C.: Association for the Study of Higher Education, 2001.

Wellman, B. "Network Analysis: Some Basic Principles." In R. Collins (ed.), *Sociological Theory.* San Francisco: Jossey-Bass, 1983.

Whitely, W., Dougherty, T. W., and Dreher, G. F. "Relationship of Career Mentoring and Socioeconomic Origin to Managers' and Professionals' Early Career Progress." *Academy of Management Journal,* 1991, *34,* 331.

Wulff, D. H., Austin, A. E., Nyquist, J. D., and Sprague, J. "The Development of Graduate Students as Teaching Scholars: A Four-Year Longitudinal Study." In D. H. Wulff, A. E. Austin, and Associates, *Paths to the Professoriate: Strategies for Enriching the Preparation of Future Faculty.* San Francisco: Jossey-Bass, 2004.

Yin, R. K. *Case Study Research: Design and Methods.* (3rd ed.) London: Sage, 2003.

VICKI L. SWEITZER *is an assistant professor of economics and management at Albion College. Her research interests include doctoral education, preparation of future faculty, mentoring, social networks, and professional identity development.*

NEW DIRECTIONS FOR TEACHING AND LEARNING • DOI: 10.1002/tl

5

Informed by theories of the academic plan, concurrent curricula, and situated curriculum, this chapter discusses how the content, sequence, and context of teaching assistant preparation programs may unintentionally interfere with research-teaching integration.

Lost in Translation: Learning Professional Roles Through the Situated Curriculum

Emily M. Janke, Carol L. Colbeck

Doctoral students trained today will soon join faculties in our nation's more than three thousand colleges and universities (Association of American Universities, 1998). The preparation these students receive while in their doctoral programs will influence the ways they prioritize research, teaching, and service. In addition, the degree to which doctoral students perceive research and teaching activities as parts of a complementary whole or as mutually exclusive activities will likely affect the extent to which future faculty become integrated or fragmented professionals. With integration, faculty may productively combine their teaching, research, and service in synergistic activities; whereas fragmentation involves compartmentalizing academic roles into discrete activities accomplished at separate times or by different people (Colbeck, 1998).

This study was funded in part by a grant from the National Science Foundation for the University of Wisconsin (Grant No. 5143G006) to support the Center for the Integration of Research, Teaching, and Learning (CIRTL). The opinions expressed here do not necessarily reflect the opinions or policies of the National Science Foundation or CIRTL, and no official endorsement should be inferred.

WILEY
InterScience®
DISCOVER SOMETHING GREAT

NEW DIRECTIONS FOR TEACHING AND LEARNING, no. 113, Spring 2008 © Wiley Periodicals, Inc.
Published online in Wiley InterScience (www.interscience.wiley.com) • DOI: 10.1002/tl.308

Current Practices for Preparing Teaching Assistants

Preparing doctoral students to be teachers and researchers is frequently left to faculty mentors. Mentoring doctoral student apprentices (Kwiram, 2006) may cultivate students' scholarly perspective and help them develop a constellation of academic skills. Unstructured or ineffective mentoring, however, may leave students underprepared for their role as teachers of undergraduate students (Austin and Wulff, 2004).

Recently, departments, institutions, and national programs have developed more structured models of doctoral preparation, attempting to provide entire cohorts of students with more sustained and sophisticated training (Wulff and Austin, 2004). Preparing Future Faculty (PPF), funded by the Council of Graduate Schools and the Association of American Colleges and Universities (AAC&U) since 1993, has awarded grants to forty-three doctoral-producing universities to implement training programs that integrate preparation for teaching and "academic citizenship as well as for research" (Gaff and Pruitt-Logan, 2002). Similarly, the Center for the Integration of Research, Teaching, and Learning (CIRTL), funded by the National Science Foundation since 2003, has developed professional development programs for doctoral students in science, technology, engineering, and mathematics (STEM). Both PPF and CIRTL seek to improve undergraduate learning by providing opportunities for future faculty to integrate their research and teaching.

In this chapter, we report findings from an evaluation of a well-intentioned effort to enhance the teaching development of first-year doctoral students in chemistry. We sought to understand how and why the program was and was not achieving its goals by exploring similarities and differences between faculty intentions and doctoral student experiences of the program. We used three curriculum theories to analyze how participation in the teaching assistant preparation program and other departmental factors influenced doctoral students' perceptions of the relative importance of teaching and research and the degree to which academic roles are integrated or fragmented. In our conclusion, we discuss how good-faith efforts in preparing future faculty for both teaching and research roles might be supported so that intended messages about the priorities of the professoriate are not lost in translation.

Theoretical Framework

Three theoretical approaches to curriculum provided lenses through which we viewed how doctoral preparation shaped the chemistry doctoral students' perceptions of academic work as integrated or fragmented: the college curriculum as academic plan (Stark and Lattuca, 1997), types of concurrent curricula (Eisner, 1979; Posner, 1995), and the situated curriculum (Gherardi, Nicolini, and Odella, 1998).

NEW DIRECTIONS FOR TEACHING AND LEARNING • DOI: 10.1002/tl

Academic Plan. An academic plan is the "total blueprint" (Stark and Lattuca, 1997, p. 9) of a curriculum and includes eight elements: *purpose* (the general goals that guide the knowledge, skills, and attitudes to be learned), *content* (the subject matter within which the learning experiences are embedded), *sequence* (an arrangement of the subject matter intended to lead to specific outcomes for learners), *learners* (information about the learners for whom the plan is devised), *instructional processes* (the instructional activities by which learning may be achieved), *instructional resources* (the materials and settings to be used in the learning process), *evaluation* (the strategies used to determine if skills, knowledge, attitudes, and behavior change as a result of the learning process), and *adjustment* (changes in the plan to increase learning based on experience and evaluation). Stark and Lattuca assert that "every curriculum includes each element of the plan . . . whether conscious or not, whether a deliberate decision has been made, or whether a default has been accepted" (p. 10). The academic plan provides a useful lens through which to evaluate components of doctoral preparation programs.

Concurrent Curricula. What teachers and advisors intend to teach via the academic plan may differ from what students actually learn (Posner, 1995). Carefully planned and artfully delivered academic plans do not always achieve the outcomes intended by faculty instructors due to the influence of additional—and sometimes competing—curricula. The *intended curriculum* of a formal doctoral program usually involves coursework, semiformal seminars, research apprenticeships with faculty mentors, and opportunities to teach undergraduates. This intended curriculum consists of the *official curriculum*, including the stated goals and objectives, content, and proposed teaching methods; the *taught curriculum*, or what and how teachers and mentors actually share knowledge and skills with students; and the *tested curriculum*, delimited by the learning outcomes for which instructors hold students accountable (Posner, 1995). An important part of students' education is also derived from the *extra curriculum*, informal but intentional learning opportunities outside formal coursework.

Even as students navigate what they will learn from the intended curriculum, they assimilate many lessons from the *hidden curriculum*, the set of expectations that shape norms for behavior and values of what is really important (Jackson, 1968). This curriculum is hidden because the messages are often transmitted and received unconsciously by instructors and students, but the lessons students learn from the hidden curriculum may last longer than any learned from the intended curriculum (Eisner, 1979; Margolis and Romero, 1998). What is not taught, the *null curriculum*, also has important consequences for students because it conveys what content and processes their instructors and mentors do and do not consider legitimate (Eisner, 1979).

The *learned curriculum*, the knowledge, skills, and attitudes students actually take away from their formal and informal learning opportunities, is mediated by students' own goals, effort, and ability (Stark and Lattuca, 1997). Students are not passive absorbers of all these concurrent curricula;

rather they subtly but consistently negotiate content, assignments, performance levels, and behavioral expectations of the intended and the hidden curricula, both formal and informal, with their instructors, mentors, and fellow students (Cuban, 1992).

Situated Curriculum. Although the situated curriculum theory was developed from an analysis of the preparation of Italian construction workers (Gherardi, Nicolini, and Odella, 1998), it can inform the professional development of doctoral students within the formal educational setting of graduate school. The situated curriculum involves the pattern of learning opportunities available to organizational newcomers and is conceptually distinct from the notion of a teaching curriculum. Newcomers gain access to the knowledge and culture of an organization through participation in an ordered set of activities and tasks. Ordered activities provide "specific modes of engagement" (p. 279) or pathways along which organizational novices may follow to increase their skills and become fully skilled, legitimate members of the organization's community. Experts tend to perpetuate the curriculum as it was taught to them by their mentors, yet newcomers experience the curriculum in a social context which is beyond the intended or formal curriculum—as well as beyond the control of the expert. Viewing learning as a series of social and cognitive activities, doctoral student preparation involves both intended and learned curricula and can be understood as a series of experiences (participation and interaction) that provide and sustain the proper context for learning (Gherardi, Nicolini, and Odella, 1998, p. 277).

Applying these three theories to a teaching assistant (TA) preparation program for doctoral students in chemistry, we sought to understand how the sequence of activities and the nature of interactions between peers and faculty may have influenced how the TAs perceived the relationship between teaching and research.

Methods

We studied a teaching assistant preparation program for doctoral students within a single chemistry department at a research-intensive university in the spring of 2006. New doctoral students were required to serve as TAs in introductory undergraduate chemistry. For this work, they received tuition remuneration, a stipend, and a grade for a one-credit course. TAs were responsible for supervising laboratory sections, answering undergraduates' questions outside of class, and grading weekly quizzes, lab reports, and notebooks. Their participation in the three-week summer TA preparation course was mandatory. The new doctoral students attended lectures about learning styles, tutoring, and ethics; evaluated each other's mock recitations; and conducted the same experiments and wrote the same reports they would later supervise for their undergraduate students. During the first semester, weekly TA meetings held by faculty instructors and an upper-level doctoral student "TA trainer" were designed to prepare TAs for teaching upcoming material, to address TAs' concerns, and to communicate general information the TAs were expected to convey to the undergraduates.

Sample and Data Collection. We conducted individual interviews with instructors (the TA trainer and five faculty) and four focus groups interviews with twelve teaching assistants (46 percent of the first year doctoral students assisting with one introductory chemistry course). All interviews were conducted by the first author. We asked the advanced doctoral student and faculty about (1) their impression of the overall goals of the program, (2) their involvement and their personal goals for the program, (3) the knowledge and skills TAs should develop from participating, and (4) whether the program included learning communities, diversity training, or assessment of one's own teaching. We asked TAs (1) what they were most interested in learning from the training for their assistantships, (2) if the program improved their confidence and ability to teach to diverse students, (3) the messages they received from faculty about teaching and research, and (4) whether they developed a sense of community or learned to assess the impact of their teaching.

Data Analysis. For this chapter, we analyzed the interview transcripts for similarities and differences between instructors' and TAs' perceptions of the goals and outcomes of the program, perceived achievements and gaps in TAs' preparation for their teaching roles, and TAs' perceptions of the messages communicated by department faculty about the relative importance and integration teaching and research.

Findings

Viewing the TA preparation program through the three curricular theoretical lenses revealed four reasons why good intentions of TA preparation program developers and instructors may be lost in translation on doctoral students: (1) the distinction made between training and education, (2) differences between learning to know and working to do, (3) the fact that the sequencing of tasks can affect the perceived risks and values of those tasks, and (4) differences between intended content and learned norms. We found that the purpose, content, and sequence of activities in the TA preparation program, as well as the department context, influenced how TAs saw themselves becoming future professionals.

Training Versus Education. A first step in shaping an academic plan is to determine the purpose of the curriculum (Stark and Lattuca, 1997). Tacit assumptions about "education" and "training" that underlie statements of purpose may influence curricular decisions and learning outcomes. For example, training implies that students learn specific tasks that they can replicate and use to solve routine problems. In contrast, education implies that students are exposed to a wide expanse of theoretical and content knowledge that they can then apply in a broad array of settings and to the solution of ill-defined problems (Posner, 1995). A training approach to preparing TAs may produce workers capable of reproducing specific lessons and standardized assessments. In contrast, an education approach might introduce principles and concepts to foster creative and flexible approaches to problem solving. TAs might be encouraged to discover creative ways to enhance diverse students' learning and to perceive such discovery as similar to the problem solving they accomplish in their basic disciplinary research. The extent to which the purpose of a teaching assistant preparation program is to train or to educate may influence how doctoral students view teaching and research.

In our study, we found that chemistry faculty members' goals for the TA preparation program emphasized technical training for teaching assistant duties. Faculty shared "tricks of the trade," including where to seek advice, how to use chalkboards and other visual equipment effectively, and how to acquire resources for experiments and teaching lectures. Similarly, chemistry doctoral students' goals for the TA preparation program were wholly oriented toward training for their teaching tasks. They viewed any information unrelated to teacher preparation as a nuisance and said that discussions and workshops on general professional development, such as getting published or presenting at conferences, were "too soon" to be helpful for their doctoral student careers. Instead, TAs said they wanted to learn the "nuts and bolts" of teaching, including classroom policies and management, expectations of the department or specific instructors with whom they would be working, techniques for using lab equipment in the chemistry courses, and practice in explaining chemistry concepts.

Teaching assistant preparation programs that focus primarily on short-term tasks and "tricks of the trade" may be part of a hidden curriculum that conveys that teaching skills are relatively mechanistic and can be learned in a short span of time. In contrast, one pursues education over an extended period of time to become a researcher.

Learning to Know, Working to Do. As prospective researchers, doctoral students engage in learning ways of *knowing*. Faculty mentors expect them to become master learners who deconstruct ill-defined problems into manageable components or questions and then address the problems by combining new knowledge with existing information. Learning to know occurs through observation and practice, as well as through self-evaluation and adjustment.

As instant teachers, the chemistry students who served as teaching assistants in their first semester of doctoral work learn ways of *doing*. Faculty instructors of record expected them to supervise undergraduate labs, to present recitations and lectures, and to grade undergraduates' assignments. Similarly, doctoral students expected training in performing specific tasks. As one TA said, "I wanted to know the specific instruments, . . . the stock room rules, and how to get items (for labs). . . . I want to know stuff like what to do if someone in my lab has an allergic reaction to latex."

Education for *knowing* or training for *doing* may influence whether students perceive the associated role with learning or working. Consequently, doctoral students may consider the role of researcher with learning and the role of teacher with working. Stereotypes of workers and learners are illustrative here. Workers are paid; learners are not paid. (Doctoral students received stipends for teaching but not research during their first year in their programs.) Workers have well-defined tasks to be completed in a relatively concise period of time; learners' tasks may be ambiguous. (TAs proctored labs and graded assignments but expected to take years to learn to do research.) Workers' actions have consequences; learners' output primarily affects their own development. (TAs' poor performance might undermine undergraduate students' grades and instructor's and department goals, but one's own failure to learn how to do research might hurt only oneself.)

Whereas the intended curriculum for preparing teaching assistants emphasized technical aspects of teaching, the null curriculum (what was not taught) included foundations of pedagogy as well as studying and assessing one's own understanding and approach to teaching (Posner, 1995). Without considering learning how to teach as a way of knowing, doctoral students may perpetuate the distinction that Burton Clark (1987) observed faculty making two decades ago: teaching is work and described as a "load," while "research" is one's own work and offers the opportunity for continued learning.

Tasks, Risks, and the Value of Teaching. The sequencing of tasks introduced in the overall doctoral program may influence how doctoral students perceive the relationship between their academic roles. Research about learning to work in context, or the situated curriculum, shows that novice workers are often prepared for full organizational participation in structured phases. Gherardi, Nicolini, and Odella (1998) observed that novice Italian construction workers first engaged in a "way-in" period of observation during which they watched master workers. This period involved little risk for the workers or the organization. The next phase involved a "practice" period of moderate risk during which novices were given limited responsibility for some tasks. Once the novices mastered these tasks, they progressed to more advanced and more complex tasks that entailed greater risk. Most training, apprenticeship, or preparation programs follow the sequence of a situated curriculum (Gherardi, Nicolini, and Odella, 1998). For example, medical students are first trained how to diagnose an illness before they are taught how to treat the patient or perform surgery; electricians are taught safety measures before they are taught how to service an electrical transformer.

In contrast, the chemistry TA preparation program structured practice before observation. Doctoral students began active training for their teaching assistant roles during the summer and before they started their chemistry coursework. They took tests to evaluate their mastery of the course content they would be teaching, conducted each of the experiments they would be proctoring, and wrote lab reports similar to the ones they would be grading in their undergraduate courses. The activities structured for them offered little or no time for observing experienced teachers. After just three weeks of training, the TAs were in charge of recitation sections and supervising lab experiments.

NEW DIRECTIONS FOR TEACHING AND LEARNING • DOI: 10.1002/tl

Thus the practice period *preceded* the way-in period, during which doctoral students could have been provided opportunities to observe and receive thoughtful guidance from advanced student colleagues or faculty mentors. As one TA said, "We skipped over the teaching aspects in training and focused more on the policies and regulations. I wanted to see a classroom, maybe sit in on one that was occurring during the summer." Expecting new doctoral student TAs to teach undergraduates without a way-in period of observation and mentoring conveyed that teaching was low-risk work of relatively minor importance. One TA explained that this sense of minimal risk and importance was reinforced by a lack of feedback about teaching. "We didn't even get feedback from our instructors until three-quarters of the way through our labs and recitations. So I was doing it wrong all of that time? OK, well, why should I change now with so little time left?" The TA perceived that faculty members' tardy feedback meant that poor teaching was of relatively little consequence to the department.

The sequencing of independent practice before the opportunity for observation and supervised and mentored practice affected some of the TAs' self-confidence for their teaching roles. One said that as a result of the TA training program, she felt "better prepared for teaching" at a large, research-intensive university but didn't feel that her teaching skills had improved. On the contrary: "I would say that maybe I am a worse teacher now," she confessed. Others felt that they were "surviving" but not excelling in their teaching roles. "The first year is all about jumping through hoops. It's boot camp. It's not viewed as important to why we are here." TAs felt that teaching was a task to endure to be able to do research in future semesters. One said, "Without us, [professors] couldn't teach. They need us as much as we need them. But teaching is at the bottom of their priority list."

Taught Content and Learned Norms.   Novices in preparation programs learn both intended and unintended messages about what it means to be a member of an occupation through the materials that are selected, the skills that are taught, and the attitudes conveyed intended by senior members. Evaluations of preparation programs frequently do not include assessments of hidden curricula regarding norms, expectations, and values, but the lessons novices learn from the hidden curriculum may have a more durable impact than lessons learned from the intended curriculum (Posner, 1995).

Faculty intended that the official chemistry TA training curriculum should emphasize the value and importance of teaching and strategies for good teaching. Their good-faith intentions seemed lost on the doctoral student TAs, in part because the TAs were learning different values from their immersion in the department's culture.

Faculty members' attitudes and allocation of physical space affected TAs' perceptions of the relationship and relative importance of teaching and research. One doctoral student pointed out that the department's research-intensive faculty were given space for an up-to-date new building while the teaching-intensive faculty remained in old facilities. He took the space allocation as an indicator of the department's priorities in which "research is king." Other TAs observed that top researchers bought out their teaching time to do more research, clearly valuing one role over the other. This suggested that teaching is a secondary activity because, as one student put it, the research university is "about pumping out papers and Ph.D. students." Another TA observed tensions between faculty over the appropriate portion of time faculty and doctoral students should spend on teaching and research. "Professors who think teaching is important are defensive—they make a big deal out of it. But there are three reasons why people still TA in their second year: they couldn't get money from the department, they wanted to TA, or they were required to TA because they passed their orals with qualifications because they didn't do well on the oral part. It's a punishment [when] it's supposed to be a learning experience." One TA's comment, in particular, revealed perceptions of dramatic fragmentation between research and teaching roles: "Why use research folks to teach? Why not use teaching folks?" So despite the intentions of the TA preparation program developers to help new doctoral students learn the basics of teaching, TAs picked up from a variety of sources in the department that teaching and research were fragmented in terms of physical space and were done by different types of faculty.

A Way of Becoming. Learning is not only a way of knowing but also a way of "becoming," based on participation in a social system of situated activities (Gherardi, Nicolini, and Odella, 1998). Given this view, "on-the-job learning is no longer equated with the acquisition of work-related bits of knowledge, but it is understood as the development of a new identity" (p. 276). Gaining membership within a group carries emotional value and significance (Hogg and Abrams, 1988; Tajfel and Turner, 1985). Conceptualized as a psychosocial as well as cognitive activity, doctoral student preparation provides not only the platform for what is to be learned but also guidelines for how to become members of the academic community. For example, after his first semester as a TA, one chemistry student said he wanted to learn more about the department's expectations of faculty for promotion and tenure. "I want to know what the shoes are that they're expected to fill." The metaphor of filling another's shoes points to the social nature of looking to the actions of others who hold advanced positions (such as tenure-line faculty) for guidance in how one should conduct oneself.

Despite messages about training versus education, work versus learning, norms, sequencing, value, and risk, the chemistry students did not necessarily view teaching as a role distinct from research. Several perceived that teaching could inform their research and that research could inform their teaching. One TA said that research helped "generate interest in teaching" because research applies concepts of basic chemistry in interesting ways. Bringing research into the classroom also makes learning more interesting, suggested a TA, when undergraduates can relate what they are learning to the real world. Another doctoral student noticed synergies between teaching and research as a result of interacting with undergraduates: "I watch lab students address problems who haven't read, and you see the steps one might go through when attacking problems for the first time. It gives me the perception of how you would approach our research." Thus some of the TAs found ways that they could integrate teaching and research from their own experiences.

Recommendations: Supporting Integrated Views of the Professoriate

What can faculty members do to preserve and support doctoral students' view of teaching as important and of teaching and research as mutually supportive and often integrated roles? One strategy for preparing doctoral students who truly value teaching is to provide a "way-in" period in which doctoral students apprentice under or work with advanced doctoral students or faculty who approach teaching as an ongoing exercise in learning and research. The approach would parallel the mentoring curriculum used in labs for preparing researchers: direct observation, reflection, working with sequentially more difficult technology and more expensive materials, and feedback on one's practice from the mentor. A teaching mentorship with a faculty member or advanced graduate student would provide opportunities through which new TAs could seek advice and support for teaching in innovative ways and for understanding the impact of their teaching on student learning.

A second strategy for improving doctoral preparation for teaching would be to incorporate readings and discussions of pedagogy into existing TA preparation programs. Pedagogy entails more than knowing how to prepare curricular materials; it includes understanding the cognitive, social, cultural, and environmental factors that affect learning and devising strategies to guide learners in constructing their own knowledge. Rather than providing simple "tricks of the trade" or lessons learned from others' experiences, TA preparation programs that approach teaching as facilitating student learning could provide a framework for preparing, presenting, evaluating, and adjusting an academic plan in a timely and effective manner.

Third, encouraging current and future faculty to study the relationship between teaching and students' learning—that is, to engage in a kind of practitioner research on their own classroom experiences—may help doctoral students conceptualize teaching and research as activities that inform each other (Connolly, Bouwma-Gearhart, and Clifford, 2007). By applying a research approach to teaching (by identifying, researching, and attempting to solve a problem), TAs might, for example, diagnose problems in case studies, thereby learning ways to assess their own work with students and improve their current and future teaching practices. The Center for the Integration of Research, Teaching, and Learning (described more fully in Chapter Six in this volume) offers the following guidelines for engaging in such activities, which CIRTL (2005) calls "Teaching-as-Research" (TAR):

1. Learning foundational knowledge (What is known about the teaching practice?)
2. Creating objectives for student learning (What do I want students to learn?)
3. Developing a hypothesis for practices to achieve the learning objectives (How can I help students succeed with the learning objectives?)
4. Defining measures of success (What evidence will I need to determine whether students have achieved learning objectives?)
5. Developing and implementing teaching practices within an experimental design (What will I do in and out of the classroom to enable students to achieve learning objectives?)
6. Collecting and analyzing data (How will I collect and analyze information to determine what students have learned?)
7. Reflecting, evaluating, and iterating (How will I use what I have learned to improve my teaching?)

Applying TAR offers current and future faculty opportunities to engage in teaching as a continuous process of discovery and change, paralleling and intersecting with their discovery through basic disciplinary research.

What students actually learn about faculty careers depends on how doctoral programs enact the purpose, content, sequence, practices, and evaluation of their overall academic plans. The social and organizational contexts of learning have powerful and profound implications for new doctoral students as they learn not only what to *know* but who to *be* as prospective faculty members. Therefore, faculty and administrators of doctoral programs should examine the unintended consequences of some current practices. The ways that their department culture values teaching and research roles, approaches responsibility, or integrates or fragments work activities will be mirrored in the attitudes and behaviors of new doctoral students as they become situated within the academic community.

References

Association of American Universities. *Committee on Graduate Education: Report and Recommendations.* Washington, D.C.: Association of American Universities, 1998.

Austin, A. E., and Wulff, D. H. "The Challenge to Prepare the Next Generation of Faculty." In D. H. Wulff, A. E. Austin, and Associates, *Paths to the Professoriate: Strategies for Enriching the Preparation of Future Faculty.* San Francisco: Jossey-Bass, 2004.

Center for the Integration of Research, Teaching, and Learning. "Teaching-as-Research: Developmental Framework." 2005. http://cirtl.wceruw.org/TARframework.pdf. Accessed Nov. 30, 2007.

Clark, B. R. *The Academic Life: Small Worlds, Different Worlds.* Princeton, N.J.: Carnegie Foundation for the Advancement of Teaching, 1987.

Colbeck, C. L. "Merging in a Seamless Blend: How Faculty Integrate Teaching and Research." *Journal of Higher Education,* 1998, *69,* 647–671.

Connolly, M. R., Bouwma-Gearhart, J. L., and Clifford, M. A. "The Birth of a Notion: The Windfalls and Pitfalls of Tailoring an SoTL-Like Concept to Scientists, Mathematicians, and Engineers." *Innovative Higher Education,* 2007, *32,* 19–34.

Cuban, L. "Curriculum Stability and Change." In P. W. Jackson (ed.), *Handbook of Research on Curriculum*. New York: Macmillan, 1992.

Eisner, E. W. *The Educational Imagination: On the Design and Evaluation of School Programs*. New York: Macmillan, 1979.

Gaff, J. G., and Pruitt-Logan, A. S. "About This Publication." In A. L. DeNeef (ed.), *The Preparing Future Faculty Program: What Difference Does It Make?* Washington, D.C.: Association of American Colleges and Universities, 2002.

Gherardi, S., Nicolini, D., and Odella, F. "Toward a Social Understanding of How People Learn in Organizations." *Management Learning*, 1998, *29*, 273–297.

Hogg, M. A., and Abrams, D. *Social Identifications: A Social Psychology of Intergroup Relations and Group Processes*. New York: Routledge, 1988.

Jackson, P. W. "The Daily Grind." In P. W. Jackson (ed.), *Life in Classrooms*. Austin, Tex.: Holt, Rinehart and Winston, 1968.

Kwiram, A. L. "Time for Reform?" In C. M. Golde and G. E. Walker (eds.), *Envisioning the Future of Doctoral Education: Preparing Stewards of the Discipline*. San Francisco: Jossey-Bass, 2006.

Lave, J., and Wenger, E. *Situated Learning: Legitimate Peripheral Participation*. New York: Cambridge University Press, 1991.

Margolis, E., and Romero, M. "'The Department Is Very Male, Very White, Very Old, and Very Conservative': The Functioning of the Hidden Curriculum in Graduate Sociology Departments." *Harvard Educational Review*, 1998, *68*, 1–32.

Posner, G. J. *Analyzing the Curriculum*. (2nd ed.) New York: McGraw-Hill, 1995.

Stark, J. S., and Lattuca, L. R. *Shaping the College Curriculum: Academic Plans in Action*. Boston: Allyn & Bacon, 1997.

Tajfel, H., and Turner, J. C. "The Social Identity Theory of Intergroup Behavior." In S. Worchel and W. G. Austin (eds.), *Psychology of Intergroup Relations*. Chicago: Nelson-Hall, 1985.

Wulff, D. H., and Austin, A. E. "Strategies to Enhance Paths to the Professoriate." In D. H. Wulff, A. E. Austin, and Associates, *Paths to the Professoriate: Strategies for Enriching the Preparation of Future Faculty*. San Francisco: Jossey-Bass, 2004.

EMILY M. JANKE is a doctoral candidate in higher education at Pennsylvania State University and a research assistant in the Center for the Study of Higher Education.

CAROL L. COLBECK is professor and dean of education at the University of Massachusetts Boston. Her research investigates how faculty integrate teaching, research, and service; how faculty teaching and organizational climate affect student learning; and how faculty balance professional and personal responsibilities.

6

This chapter describes a comprehensive program to pre-
pare science, technology, engineering, and mathematics
(STEM) doctoral students for faculty careers that inte-
grate research and education.

Strategies for Preparing Integrated Faculty: The Center for the Integration of Research, Teaching, and Learning

Ann E. Austin, Mark R. Connolly, Carol L. Colbeck

When university and college search committees select new faculty members, they hope that the newcomer will understand and support the missions of the institution and be successful in integrating components of the professorial role—including research, teaching, learning, advising, institutional citizenship, and outreach and professional service responsibilities—into a satisfying and productive career. Yet research shows that many doctoral students are not adequately prepared to handle the full range of roles that are part of academic work. Golde and Dore (2001) assert that there is a misalignment in the goals and training that occur in doctoral education and the careers that graduates will enter. In fact, research on doctoral education over the past decade has highlighted various concerns—the multiple and conflicting messages that aspiring faculty perceive about how to focus their efforts, their perceptions that they received inadequate feedback, and the lack of systematic focus in doctoral education on preparing doctoral students to teach (Austin, 2002; Lovitts, 2001; Wulff, Austin, Nyquist, and Sprague, 2004).

The research that highlights concerns about doctoral education have been coupled with programmatic efforts by doctoral-granting institutions, foundations, and national associations to develop, implement, and evaluate initiatives and strategies to prepare the next generation of faculty more fully

NEW DIRECTIONS FOR TEACHING AND LEARNING, no. 113, Spring 2008 © Wiley Periodicals, Inc.
Published online in Wiley InterScience (www.interscience.wiley.com) • DOI: 10.1002/tl.309

for the responsibilities they will assume. These efforts—such as the Carnegie Foundation for the Advancement of Teaching's Initiative on the Doctorate (Walker, 2004), the Preparing Future Faculty Program (Pruitt-Logan and Gaff, 2004), and the Woodrow Wilson Foundation's Responsive Ph.D. Program (Weisbuch, 2004)—prepare what this volume calls "integrated professionals," individuals who understand, value, and incorporate into their work a range of commitments and activities. The Center for the Integration of Research, Teaching, and Learning (CIRTL) is another example of a comprehensive programmatic strategy targeted at preparing the next generation of faculty as integrated professionals.

In this chapter, we discuss CIRTL's mission, conceptual pillars, history, and components. We also describe how the University of Wisconsin–Madison has developed its Delta Program as a prototype for CIRTL institutional activities. Third, to explore whether a CIRTL-like program at a research university can make a measurable impact on preparing integrated professionals, we offer a synopsis of the research findings to date on the impact on doctoral students who are Delta participants. Finally, we raise some questions concerning strategies for preparing faculty as integrated professionals that deserve further consideration and research. Our overall purpose in this chapter is to show how the conceptual ideas advanced in this volume about preparing integrated professionals can be effectively translated into practice in doctoral education.

The Center for the Integration of Research, Teaching, and Learning

Funded by the National Science Foundation (NSF) as one of its national centers focused on educational practice and research, CIRTL began in 2003 as a collaborative effort between the University of Wisconsin–Madison, Michigan State University, and Pennsylvania State University. Its mission has been to prepare future faculty—initially in science, technology, engineering, and mathematics (STEM) and now also in social and behavioral sciences—who are excellent teachers as well as superb researchers. The stated objective of CIRTL emphasizes its aim to influence doctoral education across the country:

> The Center for the Integration of Research, Teaching, and Learning (CIRTL) will create a model interdisciplinary professional development program in teaching and learning that will prepare graduate students, and with them postdoctoral researchers and current faculty . . . to meet the future challenges of national STEM higher education. . . . CIRTL seeks to influence graduate-through-faculty development at a significant number of research institutions throughout the nation. Developing effective methods of adapting programs successful at one research university to another is central to the CIRTL scope of work. . . . Ultimately the vision is to . . . create STEM faculties at all higher education institutions committed to ongoing improvement of student learning [CIRTL, 2003].

NEW DIRECTIONS FOR TEACHING AND LEARNING • DOI: 10.1002/tl

Several key principles have guided the development of CIRTL. First is the assumption that doctoral students should be prepared not only as researchers but also as teachers and that potential future faculty should appreciate the missions of the range of institutions in which they may work. The second assumption is that strong preparation for teaching as well as for research responsibilities will prepare doctoral graduates to be more competitive for faculty positions and give a more productive and rewarding start to their faculty careers. Furthermore, by using the skills of excellent teachers, future faculty will understand how to conceptualize and explain the broader impact of their research and therefore do well as grant seekers. Another assumption is that undergraduate education in the STEM fields will be enhanced as faculty become more effective teachers. Finally, whereas one university alone cannot improve the preparation of the nation's future faculty, CIRTL leaders assert that a group of universities working together can effect major change in the dominant preparation patterns.

Three conceptual "pillars" guide CIRTL's plans, programs, and activities: Teaching-as-Research (TAR), Learning Communities (LC), and Learning-through-Diversity (LTD). Teaching-as-Research "involves the deliberate, systematic, and reflective use of research methods to develop and implement teaching practices that advance the learning experiences and outcomes of students and teachers" (CIRTL, 2006). TAR derives from the approach that scientists take to advance knowledge—that is, creating objectives, developing hypotheses, framing questions to explore the hypotheses, gathering data, analyzing the data, drawing conclusions, and taking actions based on the conclusions. In each CIRTL program, participants use a similar approach to examine and improve their teaching and their students' learning. TAR is similar to the Scholarship of Teaching and Learning, defined by the Carnegie Foundation for the Advancement of Teaching and advanced in conferences and scholarly articles (Hutchings and Clarke, 2004), Classroom Research (Angelo and Cross, 1993; Cross and Steadman, 1996), and action research models (Reason, 2007; Stringer, 2007), but the designation Teaching-as-Research seems to have particular resonance for scientists and engineers.

A second pillar guiding CIRTL courses, activities, and programs is a commitment to a Learning Community approach to fostering and supporting learning. CIRTL (2006) defines learning community as "the process by which individuals come together to achieve learning goals." Learning communities create situations in which participants have meaningful interactions with others that support their achieving the learning goals of a course or program. Learning experiences in a learning community are typically collaborative and involve making implicit and explicit connections that link learning experiences to life situations beyond the specific course or program. In learning communities, diversity is welcomed and recognized as an important ingredient that informs the learning experience in significant ways. Overall, in a CIRTL learning community context, graduate students, postdoctoral scholars, and faculty work together to learn and generate new understandings about teaching and learning.

The concept of Learning-through-Diversity emerged as a third core pillar within the first year of CIRTL's existence. LTD is based on a recognition that "excellence and diversity are necessarily intertwined" and that learning is enhanced by building on the diverse backgrounds, skills, and experiences of all learners in a group (CIRTL, 2006). Because educational situations do not always encourage the complete success of all learners, CIRTL emphasizes explicit attention to creating intentionally equitable learning environments. This commitment involves helping graduate students, postdocs, and faculty learn more about the diversity of their students; learn to recognize, respect, and build on the diversity that their students bring in ways that enrich the learning of all participants; and become proficient in using curricular, teaching, and assessment practices that recognize diversity and encourage learning for all students.

Initially, CIRTL developed a prototype program for preparing future faculty who value and have the skills to excel at both teaching and research at the University of Wisconsin–Madison. Michigan State and Penn State have also been early collaborators, developing plans for their own institutional models to prepare future faculty that incorporate the three pillars in ways appropriate for their unique university cultures. During its third year, in 2006, CIRTL expanded into a network of seven universities, adding Howard University, Vanderbilt University, the University of Colorado at Boulder, and Texas A&M to the original three. These research universities have formed a learning community (modeling CIRTL's Learning Community pillar) to function as a group of peers that are experimenting (modeling the TAR pillar) with strategies to prepare future faculty. While each is developing its own models for doctoral student development appropriate for its own context, culture, and history, the CIRTL Network universities share similar goals for preparing future faculty who demonstrate excellence in teaching and research, for integrating the core CIRTL pillars into their doctoral professional development programs, and for sharing what they are learning about the effectiveness of their programs and strategies. The CIRTL Network also provides opportunities for graduate students, postdoctoral scholars, and faculty members to interact across the institutions through involvement in meetings, workshops, and online courses (an example of the pillar of Learning Through Diversity).

CIRTL also organized and supported a Diversity Institute whose members have developed and identified resources and compiled a bibliography on learning and teaching through diversity, written a case book and a resource book, developed a self-guided workshop on diversity issues, and offered related workshops and presentations. The 2005 CIRTL National Forum titled "Addressing the Student Learning Experience: Achieving Diversity in STEM Disciplines" convened administrators, faculty, and students interested in recognizing and building on learners' diversity to foster effective learning experiences. Another national forum is planned in the near future.

The Delta Program at the University of Wisconsin–Madison

At the University of Wisconsin–Madison (UW–Madison), CIRTL supported the development of the Delta Program in Research, Teaching, and Learning, the prototype implementation of CIRTL's Professional Development Program. Delta is essentially the laboratory for CIRTL, modeling the TAR approach to improving teaching and learning by developing hypotheses and questions about the preparation of future professionals, gathering and analyzing data in response to the questions, and developing conclusions and lessons to inform further practice. Since 2003, Delta has offered graduate students, postdoctoral researchers, academic staff, and faculty—especially those in science, technology, engineering, mathematics, and social and behavioral sciences—many opportunities for learning to integrate their research and teaching roles. All Delta programs explicitly build on the three pillars of CIRTL. (For further information, go to http://www.delta.wisc.edu.)

Currently, Delta offers an array of opportunities for doctoral students in STEM and social and behavioral disciplines, including courses, workshops, programs, roundtable discussions, and dinner gatherings. Six semester-long courses include Teaching Science and Engineering: The College Classroom, Informal Education: A Practicum for Scientists, Effective Teaching with Technology, Instructional Materials Development, Diversity in the College Classroom, and Teaching Science and Engineering: International Faculty, International Students. Delta also offers three small-group facilitated programs, including one called Creating a Collaborative Learning Environment (CCLE). This program enables groups of seven to nine graduate students, postdocs, and faculty members to explore teaching- and learning-related topics together. The Expeditions in Learning program provides the opportunity for groups of eight participants to visit teaching and learning sites around campus, such as the library, residence halls, laboratories, and different kinds of classes, and to discuss the implications of these sites for learning. The Postdoc Discussion Group, in which participants discuss career issues, is the third small-group program.

Through the Delta Internship Program, doctoral students work with faculty mentors on Teaching-as-Research projects that often include Learning Community or Learning-through-Diversity components. These internships occur either at the University of Wisconsin–Madison or at nearby two- and four-year institutions. In addition to these semester-long or yearlong opportunities, Delta offers a workshop on developing teaching and learning portfolios, workshops on writing "broader impact statements" for NSF grant proposals and CAREER Award proposals, and symposia and institutes on teaching and learning issues jointly offered with other campus units. Round-table dinners bring together all Delta participants once a month for guest speakers and informal discussion. Delta offers a certificate in research, teaching, and learning to doctoral students and postdocs who complete two graduate courses in teaching and learning, an internship, and a teaching portfolio.

All of Delta's courses and programs focus, to varying degrees, on the three CIRTL pillars: Teaching-as-Research, Learning Community, and Learning-through-Diversity. While some doctoral students, postdocs, and faculty choose to get involved in a number of activities and programs, others participate more modestly. One hallmark of Delta, and all CIRTL institutional programs, is the option to enter at various points and participate at either low or high levels of commitment and involvement.

Through these programs, Delta strives to cultivate a vibrant interdisciplinary, intergenerational learning community that helps participants examine systematically the relationship between their teaching and their students' learning. Overall, using the language of this volume, the Delta program helps graduate students and postdoctoral scholars, as well as the faculty involved in the program, develop the knowledge, skills, and abilities that support their emergence as integrated professionals.

Impact of a Systematic Program to Prepare Integrated Professionals

What evidence do we have that a program like Delta, which is one institution's approach to professional development guided by the CIRTL mission and pillars, is contributing to the education of integrated professionals? To guide efforts to improve the preparation of future faculty and postsecondary educators, CIRTL researchers gathered campuswide data at the University of Wisconsin–Madison about the relationship between research and teaching roles of faculty and doctoral students. For example, an early needs assessment study conducted by CIRTL researchers reported that UW administrators, faculty, academic staff, and doctoral students perceived a persistent disjuncture between disciplinary research and undergraduate teaching (Millar, Clifford, and Connolly, 2004). Furthermore, a baseline survey of UW–Madison doctoral students and postdoctoral researchers in STEM fields found that although over 80 percent of graduate students and postdocs aspired to work at a research or teaching-intensive university, they had limited opportunities to engage in significant teaching experiences or to learn about postsecondary teaching and learning (Dillenburg, 2005; Dillenburg and Connolly, 2005). Although many respondents had teaching experiences that entailed grading papers or leading discussions, only about one-fourth had significant teaching experiences, such as being the primary instructor for a semester-long course that included a range of instructional responsibilities. Findings from these early studies suggested there was a clear need for activities that would better prepare doctoral students and postdocs for the full range of roles and responsibilities that full-time faculty are expected to manage.

To document Delta's impact, if any, on its target audience—namely, STEM doctoral students and postdocs—Delta administrators used a well-known model for evaluating training programs (Kirkpatrick, 1998, modified by Colbeck, 2003) as a framework for discerning the various levels at which programmatic impact can occur. The five levels of program impact and the fundamental questions each level addresses are as follows:

1. *Participation:* Who attended? What motivated them to attend?
2. *Satisfaction:* Were participants satisfied with the program? Did they get from participation what they expected?
3. *Learning:* What did participants learn? What attitudes or beliefs were acquired or changed? What skills were developed?
4. *Application:* Did participants apply and refine knowledge, attitudes, and skills in subsequent situations of authentic practice?
5. *Overall impact:* What role, if any, did participation in the program subsequently play in improving undergraduate STEM education?

CIRTL researchers and Delta administrators gathered impact data through questionnaires, interviews, and focus groups. In the following sections, we examine Delta's influence on its doctoral and postdoctoral participants' capacity for balancing and integrating research and teaching by level of impact and provide examples of our evidence.

Participation. Attendance data reveal that nearly 1,300 UW–Madison graduates through faculty have participated in Delta since 2003, of which 876 (68 percent) are graduate students ($n = 704$) and postdocs ($n = 172$). Of these, approximately 300 graduate students have enrolled in a Delta-sponsored internship, course, or program lasting a semester. Each semester, 5 percent of all STEM graduate students are involved in some kind of Delta activity on average.

Satisfaction. Since spring, 2006, all Delta course evaluation forms have included a number of common questions, including one asking about overall satisfaction. Responses indicate that more than 80 percent of participants were satisfied or extremely satisfied with their course or activity. Together, the satisfaction and attendance data suggest that Delta has attracted many of its targeted audience to various events that focus on, among other things, integrating research and teaching and that most participants in the most time-intensive activities are satisfied with their courses.

Learning. Because CIRTL's three pillars were emphasized in almost every programmatic offering, assessments of what participants learned from Delta courses and programs has focused on these key ideas. When asked to describe specific steps they would take in future teaching practice, 56 percent of course participants with just one Delta course said they would incorporate the ideas and activities of at least two of the pillars in their teaching.

Of Delta participants who had taken part in two or more Delta courses and programs, 80 percent mentioned at least two of the three Delta pillars, and 90 percent specifically expressed how they intended to apply their knowledge in their future practice (Pfund and others, 2006).

Since data collected by Delta program administrators provided a limited perspective on the three higher levels of program effects (learning, application, and overall impact), CIRTL researchers have conducted additional studies to gauge the effects of Delta on participants. For example, a 2005 survey to a random sample showed that doctoral students and postdoctoral researchers who had participated in Delta had more positive attitudes and beliefs about teaching than those who had not participated in Delta (Barger and Webb, 2006). An interview study with nearly seventy Delta participants and instructors in spring 2005 indicated that the adoption of Teaching-as-Research, one of CIRTL's pillars, helped graduate students and faculty link their disciplinary research with approaches to studying their own students' learning (Connolly, Bouwma-Gearhart, and Clifford, 2007).

CIRTL researchers are also conducting a longitudinal study of fifty-one doctoral students and postdoctoral researchers who participated in one or more Delta events or programs. By following these individuals over a three-year period, CIRTL researchers have gained a deeper understanding of what participants learn from Delta and how they may use it in practice. Findings from second-year interviews revealed that participants felt they needed more preparation for various faculty roles than their training typically included and that participating in Delta and other teaching-related professional development activities helped address their felt needs for such training (Bouwma-Gearhart, Millar, Barger, and Connolly, 2007). Gaining knowledge and skills from teaching-related professional development was the most frequently mentioned effect of participation. A number of study respondents said that they learned about pedagogical terms and resources, designing courses around learning outcomes, and systematically gathering feedback from students about how much they are actually learning. Many respondents also described changes in their attitudes about teaching, adding that as a result of their participation, they were more excited about teaching, had greater confidence about their teaching abilities, and were committed to their ongoing participation in teaching-related professional development. Respondents also emphasized the importance of joining teaching-related communities and networks through professional development activities.

Finally, interviews with Delta participants who had transitioned from training experiences at UW into new positions suggested a strong relationship between the amount of teaching-related professional development and (1) a belief that the opportunity to participate in teaching-related professional development was a factor in obtaining their new position, (2) a belief that such professional development expanded their job options, (3) a sense of teaching efficacy, (4) a desire to participate in teaching-related communities, and (5) dissatisfaction with the quality of, and access to, teaching-related networks at their new institutions. In short, the findings from CIRTL's longitudinal study suggest that Delta provides opportunities for doctoral students and postdocs to gain pedagogical knowledge, skills, and confidence; enhances their competitiveness for academic positions; and encourages their further participation in teaching-related professional development during the early career years.

Application. Because many Delta participants may not have an opportunity to apply what they have learned from programs and courses until they leave graduate school or begin a faculty position, it has been a challenge to assess whether its many participants can actually improve teaching and learning by drawing on the CIRTL pillars of Teaching-as-Research, Learning Communities, and Learning-through-Diversity. One group of participants that has such experiences, however, are those participating in Delta-sponsored internships. Forty-one Delta interns to date have designed, implemented, and analyzed Teaching-as-Research projects to address student learning challenges at the University of Wisconsin–Madison or at nearby colleges. Nearly every one obtained prior data on student knowledge, designed an intervention from research-based effective teaching strategies, collected and analyzed data on outcomes, and communicated those outcomes to the learning community (through publication in some cases). One intern described how her involvement in Delta influenced her ability to balance research and teaching responsibilities:

> I was having a severe crisis and questioning whether to continue on an academic track. I felt I could sort of handle research, but I wanted to be a professor, and the thought of teaching and putting together courses on top of research completely panicked me. . . . Delta, through its courses and internship, was a very key factor in making the professor track happen. I decided that if I was going to be a professor, I needed to do what it would take to make me feel comfortable with teaching, because if I didn't feel comfortable, I didn't want to continue.

Other evidence of Delta participants' ability to apply what they learned comes from CIRTL's longitudinal study. At the time of the second-year interviews, most of the fifty-one interviewees were still doctoral students or postdoctoral scholars, only a few of whom said that they had had an opportunity to put their knowledge and skills into practice, such as while working as a teaching assistant. Of eight participants who had transitioned to new roles, such as faculty positions, two who were teaching college courses said they were using what they had learned about Teaching-as-Research to engage students and assess their learning. A third instructor said she was not sure how much of what she had learned from Delta would be useful during her frenetic first year as an assistant professor, but she was hopeful that she could attempt some innovative teaching practices in the next year or two.

Overall Impact. Among Delta's principal aims is preparing a new generation of STEM faculty who will be both excellent researchers and effective teachers. Delta's success in educating integrated professionals is an ongoing question that we are continuing to address.

Preparing Integrated Professionals: Questions and Issues for Further Consideration

Educating the next generation of faculty is one of the very important responsibilities of the faculty and administrative leaders who work with today's doctoral students. Given the range of expectations that universities and colleges must fulfill for society, faculty should have the skills to carry out various kinds of work, including teaching, research, outreach, and institutional citizenship. Programs like Delta and initiatives at other CIRTL Network institutions and at other universities around the country offer models for addressing this responsibility. Descriptions of the strategies being developed and evaluated at other CIRTL institutions, as well as course and workshop descriptions and other resources developed through CIRTL, are posted regularly on the CIRTL Web site, http://www.wceruw.org.

The research effort to examine the impact of such programs is already providing results that contribute to improving existing programs and information for others considering their own programs. Additional interesting questions and issues deserve further consideration by institutional leaders and researchers. Attention to these questions will help refine programs to prepare future integrated professionals in ways that maximize the impact and success of these efforts.

Faculty advisors, graduate deans, and professional development specialists would benefit from knowing more about when in a doctoral program is the best time for providing professional development focused on integrating professional roles and which strategies have the most impact. Different types of professional development may be effective at different stages of doctoral education. For example, doctoral students may be more likely to take courses that focus on professional development in the first few years of their graduate work before focusing deeply on their research. On the other hand, some students (and their advisors) may prefer that the early years involve immersion in the discipline without involvement in what some might perceive as competing activities. Patterns may vary by discipline. Other important questions concern the degree and nature of impact from participation in workshops, courses, or informal gatherings. The usefulness and impact of each type of program may vary, depending on students' disciplines, years toward the degree, and levels of interest. Do graduate students benefit more from professional development that includes students from a range of disciplines or when participants are from the same discipline? A question that is of particular interest to CIRTL leaders and under study by CIRTL researchers is the issue of how much professional development is "enough." What is the difference in impact for students who participate deeply in professional development compared to those who are able to participate only modestly or occasionally? This question is particularly important because graduate deans and faculty advisors want to provide effective professional development while supporting students in timely completion of their degrees.

The attitudes of disciplinary faculty are an implementation issue to consider when designing effective professional development efforts. Doctoral students sometimes find that their faculty advisors are reluctant to allow them to engage in activities outside the disciplines (Austin, 2002; Wulff, Austin, Nyquist, and Sprague, 2004). Particularly in the STEM fields, students may be required to give ongoing, daily attention to laboratory work and research. Deans, project leaders, and professional development specialists who design programs to educate doctoral students as integrated professionals need to find ways to enlist the support and interest of disciplinary faculty. Furthermore, professional development activities should be offered and organized in ways that do not interfere or impede students' disciplinary commitments.

Another implementation concern involves the graduates' transition to full-time professional roles. Moving from awareness to enactment of the roles and responsibilities of integrated professional work can be daunting. Ph.D.-granting institutions, employing institutions, and disciplinary and professional societies can facilitate the transition. Ph.D. institutions can offer professional development opportunities like those discussed in this chapter. Employing institutions can offer further professional development programs, mentoring from department chairs, and opportunities for new faculty to interact with each other across disciplines. Some employing institutions may not value the notion of an integrated professional, so doctoral students should have some guidance while still in graduate study about how to assess potential employers' priorities with their own career commitments. Finally, disciplinary and professional associations can foster discussions at conferences and in publications about what it means to be an integrated professional in the particular discipline and can highlight effective strategies to achieve this goal.

New and future faculty who know how to manage and integrate their roles and responsibilities are likely to make significant contributions and find considerable satisfaction in their work. Developing, offering, and evaluating institutional strategies to help doctoral students develop such understandings and skills deserve thoughtful and systematic attention by graduate deans, faculty advisors, and professional development specialists.

References

Angelo, T. A., and Cross, K. P. *Classroom Assessment Techniques: Handbook for College Teachers*. San Francisco: Jossey-Bass, 1993.

Austin, A. E. "Preparing the Next Generation of Faculty: Graduate Education as Socialization to the Academic Career." *Journal of Higher Education*, 2002 73, 94–122.

Barger, S., and Webb, N. "Delta Participation and the Attitudes, Beliefs, and Professional Development Experiences of Doctoral Students and Postdoctoral Researchers in

Science, Technology, Engineering, and Mathematics (STEM) at the University of Wisconsin–Madison." Madison: Center for the Integration of Research, Teaching, and Learning, University of Wisconsin–Madison, 2006.

Bouwma-Gearhart, J., Millar, S. B., Barger, S. S., and Connolly, M. R. "Doctoral and Post-doctoral STEM Teaching-Related Professional Development: Effects on Training and Early Career Periods." Paper presented at the annual meeting of the American Educational Research Association, Chicago, Apr. 2007.

Center for the Integration of Research, Teaching, and Learning (CIRTL). "Strategic Plan." Submitted to the National Science Foundation, June 23, 2003.

Center for the Integration of Research, Teaching, and Learning (CIRTL). "Annual Report (April 2005–March 2006)." Submitted to the National Science Foundation, 2006.

Colbeck, C. L. "Measures of Success: An Evaluator's Perspective." Presentation at the CIRTL Forum, Center for the Integration of Research, Teaching and Learning, Madison, Wisc., Nov. 2003.

Connolly, M. R., Bouwma-Gearhart, J. L., and Clifford, M. A. "The Birth of a Notion: The Windfalls and Pitfalls of Tailoring an SoTL-Like Concept to Scientists, Mathematicians, and Engineers." *Innovative Higher Education,* 2007, *32,* 19–34.

Cross, K. P., and Steadman, M. *Classroom Research: Implementing the Scholarship of Teaching.* San Francisco: Jossey-Bass, 1996.

Dillenburg, P. "A Report on Attitudes and Aspirations Related to College Teaching Held by Postdoctoral Employees in Science, Technology, Engineering, and Mathematics at the University of Wisconsin–Madison." Madison: Center for the Integration of Research, University of Wisconsin–Madison, 2005.

Dillenburg, P., and Connolly, M. "A Report on Attitudes and Aspirations Related to College Teaching Held by Doctoral Students in Science, Technology, Engineering, and Mathematics at the University of Wisconsin–Madison." Madison: Center for the Integration of Research, Teaching, and Learning, University of Wisconsin–Madison, 2005.

Golde, C., and Dore, T. "At Cross Purposes: What the Experiences of Doctoral Students Reveal About Doctoral Education. Philadelphia: Pew Charitable Trusts, 2001. http://www.phd-survey.org/report.htm. Accessed Nov. 30, 2007.

Hutchings, P., and Clarke, S. E. "The Scholarship of Teaching and Learning: Contributing to Reform in Graduate Education." In D. H. Wulff, A. E. Austin, and Associates, *Paths to the Professoriate: Strategies for Enriching the Preparation of Future Faculty.* San Francisco: Jossey-Bass, 2004.

Kirkpatrick, D. L. *Evaluating Training Programs: The Four Levels.* (2nd ed.) San Francisco: Berrett-Koehler, 1998.

Lovitts, B. *Leaving the Ivory Tower: The Causes and Consequences of Departure from Doctoral Study.* Lanham, Md.: Rowman & Littlefield, 2001.

Millar, S. B., Clifford, M. A., and Connolly, M. R. "Needs Assessment Study: Professional Development in Teaching at the University of Wisconsin–Madison." Madison: Center for the Integration of Research, Teaching, and Learning, University of Wisconsin–Madison, 2004.

Pfund, C., and others. *The Delta Program in Research, Teaching, and Learning.* Madison: University of Wisconsin–Madison, 2006.

Pruitt-Logan, A. S., and Gaff, J. "Preparing Future Faculty: Changing the Culture of Doctoral Education." In D. H. Wulff, A. E. Austin, and Associates, *Paths to the Professoriate: Strategies for Enriching the Preparation of Future Faculty.* San Francisco: Jossey-Bass, 2004.

Reason, P. *The SAGE Handbook of Action Research.* Thousand Oaks, Calif.: Sage, 2007.

Stringer, E. *Action Research in Education.* Upper Saddle River, N.J.: Prentice Hall, 2007.

Walker, G. E. "The Carnegie Initiative on the Doctorate: Creating Stewards of the Discipline." In D. H. Wulff, A. E. Austin, and Associates, *Paths to the Professoriate: Strategies for Enriching the Preparation of Future Faculty.* San Francisco: Jossey-Bass, 2004.

Weisbuch, R. "Toward a Responsive Ph.D.: New Partnerships, Paradigms, Practices, and People." In D. H. Wulff, A. E. Austin, and Associates, *Paths to the Professoriate: Strategies for Enriching the Preparation of Future Faculty*. San Francisco: Jossey-Bass, 2004.

Wulff, D. H., and Austin, A. E. (eds.). *Paths to the Professoriate: Strategies for Enriching the Preparation of Future Faculty*. San Francisco: Jossey-Bass, 2004.

Wulff, D. H., Austin, A. E., Nyquist, J. D., and Sprague, J. "The Development of Graduate Students as Teaching Scholars: A Four-Year Longitudinal Study." In D. H. Wulff, A. E. Austin, and Associates, *Paths to the Professoriate: Strategies for Enriching the Preparation of Future Faculty*. San Francisco: Jossey-Bass, 2004.

ANN E. AUSTIN *holds the Dr. Mildred B. Erickson Distinguished Chair in Higher, Adult, and Lifelong Education at Michigan State University. Her research focuses on faculty careers and professional development, the preparation of future faculty, teaching and learning issues, academic workplaces, and organizational change and transformation in higher education.*

MARK R. CONNOLLY *is a researcher and evaluator with the Wisconsin Center for Education Research at the University of Wisconsin–Madison. He studies STEM education reform efforts, postsecondary teaching and learning, graduate education, and practitioner theorizing.*

CAROL L. COLBECK *is professor and dean of education at the University of Massachusetts in Boston. Her research investigates how faculty integrate teaching, research, and service; how faculty teaching and organizational climate affect student learning; and how faculty balance professional and personal responsibilities.*

7

A historian chronicles her department's efforts to reorient its graduate program to prepare students pragmatically for their careers.

Career Preparation for Doctoral Students: The University of Kansas History Department

Eve Levin

Under the auspices of the Carnegie Initiative on the Doctorate (CID), the Department of History at the University of Kansas recast its doctoral program to emphasize career preparation. Its creative approach has earned the department national visibility. In this chapter, I describe how the department came to reenvision graduate education, how we managed the process of change, and what innovations we instituted to launch our students into the profession as capable "stewards of their discipline," to use CID language. As cochair of the department's CID committee and its director of graduate studies, I participated in the development and implementation of the redesigned program.

The KU History Department in Fall 2003

As the "Harvard of the Plains," the University of Kansas (KU) is a research university that prides itself on academic excellence. Like many state institutions, KU has had to achieve prominence in the face of uneven financial and political governmental support. The Kansas state motto, "Ad astra per aspera"—"To the stars through adversity"—describes the university's situation as well.

For nearly eighty years, the History Department at the University of Kansas has offered the doctoral degree. It had long-standing national preeminence in several areas, including military, medieval, Latin American, and Russian and eastern European history, as well as in the emerging field of environmental history. Over a dozen assistant professors recently joined the department, giving it a sizable young and savvy cohort. New senior hires in the medieval and Russian and eastern European fields replenished strength after retirements. The department's thirty-five faculty members spanned chronological periods from antiquity to the contemporary and most geographical regions. Ph.D. students typically chose one major and two minor fields.

The department had about ninety graduate students; a lax policy on enrollment made a precise count impossible. A majority had regional ties, although the department did attract students, particularly in its "signature" fields, from other parts of the country and from abroad. Compared to peer institutions, the KU History Department enrolled a significant number of nontraditional students—individuals who had pursued other vocational directions for a decade or more before graduate study. Among the nontraditional students, military officers were the largest component, including from the Command and General Staff College at Fort Leavenworth, career officers slated for future employment at West Point or the Air Force Academy, and reservists. A few nontraditional students pursued their degrees part-time. Except for active-duty officers and some nontraditional students, most sought financial support. The department offered graduate teaching positions only for five years. Time to degree, however, averaged over ten years—at least a year more than the national standard. Although a few students intended to pursue a terminal M.A. degree, most anticipated completing the Ph.D. Except for a few military officers and nontraditional students, most hoped to secure teaching positions at four-year colleges or universities upon graduation.

Overall, the department was solid, ranking in the second quartile in the *U.S. News and World Report* and National Research Council rankings. Structurally, its program did not diverge from the norms of the discipline. It graduated on average eight Ph.D.'s per year, and most eventually landed desired positions. We perceived no crisis in how we trained our graduate students; in a 2002 self-study, the department assessed itself as "very good."

Dispelling Myths

When the department was selected for the Carnegie Initiative on the Doctorate in August 2003, few members realized what it entailed. The impetus to apply came from the university's central administration rather than the department. The provost, David Shulenburger, urged Carl Strikwerda, the associate dean of the College of Liberal Arts and Sciences, to apply on behalf of his home department, History. Department Chair Thomas Lewin and several faculty members contributed to the application. Some members suspected that the Carnegie Initiative would involve impositions in department matters from the Carnegie Foundation or the dean's office and boy-cotted it. Others lost interest when they learned that the CID did not include a transfer of funds to the department. Nonetheless, Strikwerda assembled a committee of eight faculty and two graduate students who had expressed interest. Membership changed slightly over the first year, but the committee represented a cross section of the department in several ways. The faculty came from all three professorial ranks and included both new-comers and longtime department members. Graduate students included both twenty-somethings and older individuals. The ethnically diverse com-mittee included an African American, a Hispanic American, and a Native American.

The CID committee became the place in which innovative ideas arose and fermented. Outside the department's established governing structures, the committee was not distracted from its creative work by ordinary duties, and it drew on many sources of inspiration. The department's 2002 self-study and external reviews from 1998 and 2003 pointed out strengths and weaknesses. External evaluators praised the intellectual vitality of the department, with its "remarkable array of individual faculty strength across the board," and "the quality and energy of the graduate students." But they noted a waning sense of community, cumbersome program administration, and widespread disgruntlement over funding.

A recent report by the American Historical Association, *The Education of Historians for the Twenty-First Century* (Bender, Katz, Palmer, and the Committee on Graduate Education of the American Historical Association, 2004) presented current issues concerning graduate education. It, along with essays produced for the CID (Golde and Walker, 2006), taught us that our problems—time to degree and attrition, field definition, appropriate career preparation, funding—afflicted most of our peer institutions as well (Maki and Borkowski, 2006). We encountered this commonality of experi-ence again when we met CID partner history departments at the Carnegie Foundation's convenings and American Historical Association workshops for graduate directors.

From Carnegie Foundation mentors, we learned the concept of prepar-ing "stewards of the discipline" and the value of "backward design" (Maki and Borkowski, 2006). They directed us to formulate a portrait of our ideal Ph.D. recipient. We enumerated the traits we hoped to impart to our students during their degree work: knowledge of the discipline, research experience, career management, teaching skills, and professional etiquette. Dan Bern-stein, of KU's own Center for Teaching Excellence, gave us further guidance.

In January 2004, we sent a survey to department faculty, students, and alumni, asking open-ended questions about their perception of the pro-gram's advising, educational quality, and career preparation. Response rates were disappointing: under 20 percent for current students and alumni and only 40 percent for faculty. Nonetheless, the answers were revealing. Stu-dents and alumni affirmed that our department taught them well how to function as professionals; most faculty said that it did not. But when asked about preparation for careers (at research universities, at teaching colleges, and in nonacademic positions), large majorities of current students and alumni indicated that the program prepared them inadequately (Maki and Borkowski, 2006; Golde and Dore, 2001; Nyquist and others, 1999). However, an overwhelming majority of KU faculty thought that they prepared their students well for academic positions. Most respondents said Ph.D. training should take five to six years—a sharp contrast to the department mean of ten years.

An e-mail from a recent alumnus, an assistant professor, galvanized the committee's discussion of career preparation. He wrote:

> I'm mainly teaching lower-level courses now, but I've figured out how to teach things I want to teach instead of the surveys over and over. Meanwhile, I'm coordinating our new program in Global Studies, an interdisciplinary major with tracks in History/Politics and Latin American Culture. I've done things I never dreamed about in graduate school: devised a marketing plan and assessment documents, created a program brochure, operated a budget, and created a 17-person advisory council made of academics, lawyers and corporate types. Maybe the History Department would want to consider creating a graduate seminar (or a series of workshops) to expose students to this sort of thing.

This cogent message led the committee to consider the range of faculty roles and how often professors must draw together their expertise in teaching, research, service, and life skills to function successfully in academic institutions.

Mobilizing Forces for Change

Historians tend to be conservative academically. They are prone to see the value of established ways and to undertake change slowly. Because their research tends to be highly individualistic, they are reluctant to require their colleagues to conform to a single set of rules. At KU, faculty advisors were accustomed to directing their students as they chose. In most professors' conception, the problems in our program stemmed from systemic, extra-departmental causes—particularly inadequate funding. Nobody anticipated an influx of money, and an air of resignation pervaded the department.

The KU History Department clearly wasn't broken, so why, many of its members wondered, should we try to "fix it"? Members of the department's CID team, however, were self-selected by their willingness to envision change. One of our first revelations was that "it's not all about money." Most curricular and administrative changes could be cost-neutral. Much professional enrichment could be accomplished for no more than the cost of photocopies and refreshments.

New Directions for Teaching and Learning • DOI: 10.1002/tl

Solid data—recruitment, attrition, time to degree, fields of study, post-graduation placement—proved to be a powerful force for change. Many departmental myths were simply untrue. We thought that completing the master's degree on the way to the Ph.D. caused students substantial delays, but the data revealed no correlation. We believed that most students completed their comprehensive examinations within a year of completing coursework, but in fact, the median was more than two years. We were under the impression that most of our graduates ended up at two-year and regional colleges or in nonteaching positions. In fact, 58 percent found academic teaching positions at four-year institutions around the country. Another 10 percent were employed as professional historians at nonacademic institutions, and 7 percent worked in academic administrative positions. Many military students remained in the armed services after graduation. These data gave us a better picture of our students and helped us distinguish successful aspects of our program from those that needed change.

In April of our first year in the CID, the Carnegie team enlisted faculty of the department in envisioning innovations in an all-day retreat. All but three department members attended. Conscious of how physical space can affect participants, we arranged to meet at the Dole Institute, an elegant campus facility that houses Robert Dole's vice-presidential library. In a setting that epitomized the public value of historical study, we considered what we would like to change about our graduate program and what we would like to keep. A colleague from the Slavic Department, Maria Carlson, served as moderator, so all faculty members could participate equally. We first "vented" about problems; then we began to consider what kind of program we would create if we could. We agreed that our students were capable of high-level work and on the importance of preparing them pragmatically for their careers. By day's end, we felt energized and positive about the department's future. We had generated a number of innovative practical ideas, most notably the portfolio examination (to be explained shortly).

To enact changes, the department needed to overcome its aversion to conflict. Becky Robinson, a nontraditional student who had managed transitions in the corporate world, brought her expertise to bear. She and I went down a list of faculty members—who was fully on board, who was open but cautious, who was neutral, who was wary. Which CID committee members could most easily approach potential opponents and allay their fears? Meanwhile, student members of the team, who were also active members of the department's History Graduate Students Organization, put to rest the anxieties of their compatriots. Making the program better, Becky argued with her business sense, would enhance the quality and therefore the marketability of their degrees.

Graduate students became the strongest proponents of proposed innovations. By KU tradition and university rules, students hold voting positions on most committees, where the graduate students spoke in support of our proposals. Over the next two and a half years, the department implemented

New Directions for Teaching and Learning • DOI: 10.1002/tl

numerous improvements. In each case, a majority of faculty voted in favor; with the student votes, the motions passed by comfortable margins. In the second year of the CID, I became the department's director of graduate studies and could introduce innovations that involved procedural rather than policy changes.

The Innovations

Our innovations all advanced specific goals in training students to be professional historians, addressed deficiencies in the current program, and could be implemented without new resources, either monetary or personnel.

Starting Right: Admissions and Funding. The CID team recognized that our graduates' career success begins when we admit students who have the potential to succeed. Yet our admissions philosophy and system were not designed to recruit the best students. While many peer institutions offered five-year packages of fellowships and teaching assistantships, we promised most candidates no more than a place on the alternate list for a graduate teaching assistantship (GTA). To enroll an entering class of ten to twelve students with such stingy offers, the department admitted forty to fifty applicants—most of the pool. Our external evaluators chided us for "act[ing] on the presumption that applicants must show that they are unqualified to be denied admission." They urged us to admit only the best-qualified students.

The key to meeting the external evaluators' target rested in solving the funding conundrum. Unfunded students, we knew, drop out at high rates, and the best-qualified applicants would go elsewhere if we failed to offer them funding (Council of Graduate Schools, 2004; Golde, 2000; Lovitts, 2001). However, we already had more current student contenders than we had GTA positions, and we were loath to deprive current students—even those who failed to thrive—to redirect the GTAs for recruiting.

Although the problem seemed intractable, a close budget analysis revealed that extant funds would nearly suffice if managed with greater sophistication. We urged current students to take advantage of funding opportunities in area studies centers and the Humanities and Western Civilization program that would enhance their professional profiles. Then we overbooked departmental GTA offers by one-third for prospective students and by 10 percent for current students, confident that attrition would occur. Newly able to provide all students who needed funding with support, we advertised this fact to prospective applicants. Our candidate pool increased in size and quality, our admissions became much more selective, and our entering class numbers remained stable.

While funding was an essential component in recruiting, we also considered how to recognize promising future professionals from their applications. Because we value our programmatic diversity, we did not want to fall into the elitist trap of automatically favoring students with high GRE scores coming from prominent colleges and universities. So we scrutinized applicants' personal statements, CVs, and writing samples for indications that applicants understood what professional historians do, appreciated the dedication necessary to earn an advanced degree, had the necessary background in history courses and foreign languages, and fit with KU's strengths. We implemented a two-stage process: faculty field committees pull out the most promising applicants in their areas, and a department-wide committee makes the final selection. This system guarantees that the department takes in the right number of highly qualified students and that every student has an advisor from the moment of admission.

Facilitating the Formation of Mentoring Bonds. Studies affirm the centrality of the advisor-student relationship to graduate students' success (Golde, 2005). Even after graduation, dedicated advisors continue to aid their former students' careers. Although the KU History Department prided itself on its attentive mentoring of graduate students, majorities of students, alumni, and faculty in our survey commented that advising could be uneven. Their responses hinted at a systemic reason: mandated formal reviews of students' performance had fallen into disuse. When the university registrar changed over to online enrollment in the 1990s, students no longer needed to file a plan of study or get their advisor's signature in order to register. Even the most attentive advisors often knew few specifics about their students' progress. Few bothered to file written assessments of their students, except in connection with department GTA funding when they accentuated the positive and disguised weaknesses. The department could no longer identify specific students' advisors, fields, or progress to degree.

When I became director of graduate studies, I made reestablishing formalities of advising a priority. When I write to incoming students in the spring before they start, I provide their advisor's name and contact information. Each incoming student is also paired with a peer mentor—a successful established student.

To maintain communication among students, advisors, and the graduate office, I revived old reporting requirements. Students must once again file progress reports at the end of each semester, listing courses taken and attainment of other benchmarks of progress, including portfolio checks with the advisor and, for "all but dissertations" (ABDs), chapters submitted. I reinstituted an annual review separate from GTA funding, providing advisors with their students' progress reports, internal transcripts, and an updated copy of our department's graduate handbook to encourage a thorough assessment. Faculty file a report in our graduate office that the student can read. Every summer, I review each student's file and send letters when I spot anomalies. Sometimes they and their advisors are grateful. I would like to have this responsibility institutionalized in a committee's duties so that oversight does not depend solely on the graduate director's vigilance.

In addition to promoting student-advisor relationships, I encourage graduate students to think in terms of mentoring teams. The professor who guides their research need not be the only one who helps them prepare for the job market or who provides encouragement. At orientation, I give new students a form listing various mentoring roles and encourage them to find individuals to fill those roles. The department mandates teaching mentors for GTAs, and we encourage students to affiliate with someone other than their own advisor. As graduate director, I provide backup advising, rules clarification, problem solving, and a ready supply of chocolate.

Updating the Disciplinary Foundation. The department had required one course, History 805: The Nature of History, of all M.A. and Ph.D. students. It had originally been conceived, decades before, as a survey of the main historiographical schools of western European and American scholarship, with philosophy of history and methodology components. However, the advent of area studies in the 1960s, of social history in the 1970s, of gender studies in the 1980s, and of postmodern theory in the 1990s made the emphasis on "great dead white male historians" outdated.

The CID committee looked at how peer departments used their fundamental course to orient first-semester graduate students to the historical profession and to help them develop intellectual community. Our external referees recommended a similar reconfiguration. Committee members devised several versions of History 805 syllabi, some focusing on preparation for research, others on teaching. No consensus emerged.

Meanwhile, the two new senior hires, first Steven Epstein and then me, inherited responsibility for teaching History 805. Department tradition empowered faculty members to design their courses as they saw fit. Our versions of History 805 incorporated many features the CID team had endorsed: community building for first-year students, orientation to our program and to the historical profession in general, acquaintance with research tools and methods, "cultural literacy" about the varieties of history and their dissemination, career planning, and professional ethics.

The course remains controversial, with some faculty calling for a unified syllabus (without agreeing what should be included in it), while others want the professor teaching the course to be able to cast it as he or she prefers. Student response is mixed. Most students agree that substantial parts of the course are useful for their classmates if not for themselves. Many do not put the same level of effort into History 805 as courses in their subfields, suggesting that they regard it as tangential rather than fundamental. However, the discussion itself spurred the department to think seriously about what our students need to know from the beginning to achieve ultimate career success.

Charting the Milestones of Success: The Progress Grid. The primary impetus of the design of the Progress Grid—a year-by-year timetable listing when students should meet programmatic requirements—was not career-related. Instead, the CID team crafted the grid in response to two external pressures: first, from the university administration, to reduce the department's excessive time to degree, and second, from the department's graduate students, who sought clear guidelines on how the faculty evaluated progress for the purpose of appointing GTAs.

NEW DIRECTIONS FOR TEACHING AND LEARNING • DOI: 10.1002/tl

The grid lays out what programmatic milestones a graduate student should meet year by year. Milestones include required courses, numbers of credit-hours, examinations, and foreign language certifications. The grid establishes a threshold GPA for satisfactory performance and prohibits students from carrying incompletes in courses. The grid lays out a five- or six-year degree program, depending on whether the student enters with a B.A. or an M.A. It counters the prevailing tendency to think of Ph.D. work as open-ended, something that "takes however long it takes."

When the Progress Grid was first introduced in fall 2004, a vocal segment of the faculty opposed it. Some wanted a sort of "no graduate student left behind" standard that all students could meet. Others worried that it would prevent them from advising their students to follow a different path toward the degree. Consequently, the grid has not become policy; students suffer no penalty for failing to meet its standards. At the same time, students and faculty have found the grid to be useful for differentiating between students who are "doing fine" and those whose progress is comparatively slow. When students do not meet grid norms, advisors and the graduate committees look more closely. If students have no compelling intellectual or personal reason for the delay, we advise them to leave the program.

The Progress Grid has a career dimension as well. By setting up a five- or six-year time frame for degree completion with intermediate deadlines, the grid orients future professors to a tenure clock of analogous length. Our graduates who take tenure-track faculty positions will face unforgiving standards of progress. By completing their Ph.D.'s expeditiously, they can assure prospective employing institutions that they will be qualified for tenure when the time comes.

Outside the Classroom: Engaging Students in the Profession. At a faculty-only session at the first Carnegie History convening, we regaled each other with tales of the "eureka!" moments when we first recognized that we were professional historians. One of our Carnegie Foundation hosts pointed out that not a single incident had occurred in a classroom setting. The lesson was clear: most professionalization does not take place within the established curriculum.

KU already offered graduate students a wide array of professional experiences, including committee service, conference participation, career-seeking information, and teaching opportunities. However, students' participation in these activities was haphazard; many did not recognize their value. So the CID team composed a "professionalization agenda"—listing the kinds of noncurricular professional activities students should seek out and when in their graduate careers they should do so. It includes such items as "attend an academic conference" in year 1 and "publish a book review, encyclopedia article, abstract, or translation" in year 4. Some items are service-related, such as "deliver a guest lecture" in year 2 or "take a position on a department committee" in year 3. As part of developing a professional identity, the agenda recommends "join professional associations" in year 2,

NEW DIRECTIONS FOR TEACHING AND LEARNING • DOI: 10.1002/tl

"network with established scholars" in year 3, and "practice mock interviews" in year 5.

The History Graduate Students Organization has taken the lead in organizing workshops on aspects of professionalization, in recruiting students into service experiences, and in disseminating information about opportunities.

Matching Skills and Purposes: The Foreign Language Policy. The department had long recognized that foreign language acquisition frequently impeded students' progress to the degree. For specialists in non-U.S. history fields, mere elementary reading knowledge—our department's standard, shared with most of its peers—no longer sufficed. To flourish in their careers, students need high-level foreign language skills—reading, speaking, and writing—that permit them to participate fully in professional communities abroad. Such skills, we knew, could hardly be attained if students began language study in graduate school. Meanwhile, students in the U.S. field fumed about having to study a foreign language merely to check off a requirement.

In designing a new foreign language policy, our first question became "What role will this language play in the student's professional work?" Faculty field committees determine which languages (one or two) their students need and at what level. In non-U.S. fields, we now demand that prospective students demonstrate a "usable reading capacity" in their primary research language to qualify for admission. Thus students enter the program with the language skills needed to undertake research seminar papers in their first year—allowing us to transform that requirement (more on this shortly). The actual level of language skill we require before the Ph.D. oral is pegged to the student's intended use: reading only for archaic languages and those needed only intermittently; reading, writing, speaking, and listening for modern foreign languages in the research area.

We recognize that some foreign language study is important for humanists in general so that they grasp the connections between language and culture. We therefore insist that all graduate students, regardless of field, show experience in serious language study. Most fulfill that requirement through undergraduate coursework.

Attaining Proficiency in Scholarship: Research Seminars. After the department's 1998 external review, the M.A. thesis was replaced with two "publishable-quality" research seminar papers. External evaluators pointed out that the M.A. thesis, a work of eighty to one hundred pages, had no outlet in the current world of scholarly publishing. It also greatly increased the time to the M.A. degree and consequently to the Ph.D. Seminar papers, in contrast, resemble articles—a common genre for historians to disseminate their findings.

Although the department had set the "publishable-quality" standard, it had not defined what that standard entailed. Some faculty permitted students to fulfill the requirement with essays that used a handful of primary sources in translation or surveyed secondary literature. At the other extreme, a few faculty wanted students to prove that their papers were publishable by getting them accepted by an academic journal.

The CID team considered what we wanted students to accomplish by writing seminar papers. First, students should have the experience of becoming a "producer" of original historical knowledge, honing it in conversation with peers, and disseminating it to a wider audience. Second, the seminar papers should provide students with opportunities to explore potential dissertation topics, learning the factual narrative and the sources, discovering whether the topic was both workable and engaging. In this guise, a seminar paper could form the basis for applications for predissertation funding, the dissertation prospectus, a conference presentation, and perhaps a published article. All of these accomplishments would position students for later career success.

With these goals in mind, we altered the seminar paper requirement to read "professional-quality": a significant topic; original insight into that topic; a source base consisting of primary sources in the original language; integration into the historiographical context of the secondary literature; full scholarly citation apparatus (usually footnotes or endnotes); accurate and graceful prose style; length of twenty to sixty pages. These are the characteristics of articles considered for publication at a scholarly journal. At the same time, we recognized that few established scholars can produce a publishable work in a fifteen-week semester, starting with no knowledge of the topic and while fulfilling many other professional responsibilities. Thus the research seminar became a place where students learn about the standards of scholarly publishing and proceed toward that standard, rather than the place where they are expected to attain it.

Documenting Competence: Portfolio Examinations. We recognized that our existing system of comprehensive examinations for the Ph.D. was inefficient. With the burgeoning secondary literature, students could no longer acquire genuinely "comprehensive" knowledge; exams comprised no more than a spot check. The exams did not test whether students had the skills and talent to engage in original research. Furthermore, they emphasized undergraduate skills—writing under time pressure from memory—rather than professional ones—producing cogently argued, well-documented explications. The exams were also time-consuming (an average of two years) and a major cause of our long time to degree. The only valuable aspect of the exams was the preparatory work students undertook for them.

The portfolio, the brainchild of senior professor Don Worster, displays students' preparatory work, demonstrating that they have mastered their fields of study and know what they need to write a dissertation and enter the profession (Maki and Borkowski, 2006). Students begin compiling their portfolio in their first semester, adding and amending materials as their knowledge increases. A space limit—the size of a single three-ring binder—keeps the portfolio from growing out of bounds. The portfolio contains a CV, a professional essay in which the student defines himself or herself against the backdrop of the discipline, a dissertation prospectus, research papers, synthetic essays produced for colloquia or independently, conference papers and publications, annotated bibliographies of readings, and any other materials that show the breadth and depth of their command of their discipline, including course plans and Web site designs. The portfolio serves as the basis for the oral examination, which no longer quizzes students on factual recall but is otherwise little changed.

The portfolio offers opportunities for professionalization that written exams did not. The professional essay pushes students to enunciate how they fit into their discipline, a skill they will need often in their careers. The seminar papers and the dissertation prospectus establish a long-term research agenda. Graduates can mine the synthetic essays and annotated bibliographies for material for their class lectures. In content and format, the portfolio resembles a promotion and tenure dossier—a genre they will encounter in the future.

The portfolio also provides a means for the department to reconcile conflicting imperatives concerning the definition of major and minor fields of study. The scholarship of the historical discipline increasingly blurs the old geographical and chronological boundaries and favors comparative, thematic, and theoretical approaches. Most jobs, on the other hand, are still defined by traditional geographical rubrics. How could we best prepare our students both for scholarship and for employment? Rather than change our definitions of fields—a politically problematical prospect, given our department's governing structures—we use the professional essay in the portfolio to guide students in navigating the complexities.

Preparing for Teaching Careers. The department had long recognized that the experience in teaching that many of our graduate students acquired served them well in their later careers. In applying for teaching-intensive positions, they could demonstrate success in the classroom, instructing large numbers of students with a wide range of ability levels. However, the department did not purposefully use GTA positions to enhance graduate students' career preparation. Instead, we treated GTAs as a form of financial aid—a way for students to pay their bills—while they engaged in the "real" work of courses and dissertation writing. Through the CID process, we recognized our responsibility to prepare graduates for the teaching aspects of their career, as well as for scholarly ones.

Enhancing Teaching Opportunities. Our students usually teach for ten semesters, proceeding from roles of grader or discussion section leader to assistant instructor, where they have sole responsibility for designing the syllabus and conducting the course. In the past, GTAs tended to teach the same freshman-level surveys again and again. Now we recognize the importance of giving our GTAs opportunities to diversify their teaching portfolio by taking on a variety of courses, including advanced ones. We also encourage our students to take GTA positions in the Humanities and Western Civilization (HWC) program to gain experience in the type of "great books" courses that so many colleges offer. Nearly half of our GTAs now hold positions in HWC for part of their graduate school tenure—a development that also means that there is enough funding for all students.

NEW DIRECTIONS FOR TEACHING AND LEARNING • DOI: 10.1002/tl

GTA Workshop. Under impetus from assistant professors and experienced GTAs, this annual departmental session was recast to emphasize practical techniques and solutions to common problems. All GTAs were required to participate so that newcomers could become acquainted with old-timers and learn from them. In addition to practicalities of department policy and pedagogical methods, the workshop opens a conversation on how to balance teaching and research obligations—an issue they will face throughout their careers. The graduate students found it so useful, they requested follow-up gatherings later in the year.

Teaching Exchange. An early CID innovation was the Teaching Exchange, an ongoing conversation among faculty and graduate students about aspects of teaching. The Teaching Exchange meets about once a month during the school year, with each session devoted to a specific aspect of (usually) undergraduate education. Through the Teaching Exchange, graduate students can witness how even experienced faculty grapple with the challenges of teaching and how the department assesses student learning. They can also bring their own innovations and insights—as well as frustrations and concerns—to a receptive, knowledgeable group of colleagues.

Practical Pedagogy Course. Some of our peer departments, notably our CID partner Arizona State, have their GTAs enroll in for-credit courses focused on the pedagogical issues encountered in teaching positions. Although we admired these courses, they would be impractical for our students, who need to enroll in required courses in their fields when they are offered. At the same time, we faced another problem: when students had room in their schedules for electives, they tended to enroll in upper-level undergraduate courses in order to "get a good set of notes" in preparation for teaching a similar course after graduation. Even though faculty members teaching such courses usually assigned the graduate students more sophisticated readings and a more challenging term paper, graduate students and undergraduates made an uncomfortable mix.

Our practical pedagogy course (History 807) solves both problems. In History 807, weekly class sessions introduce students to the burgeoning literature on the college-level teaching of history. In addition, each student chooses an undergraduate history course to observe throughout the semester. In consultation with that course's instructor, the observer reads the most significant scholarly literature on the topic of the course. To fulfill the requirements of History 807, students produce an annotated bibliography of their readings and design a packet of materials—syllabus, assignments, class plans, and so on—for their own version of the course they observed. They then include both in their professional portfolios.

Commendation in Teaching Preparedness. We were intrigued by departments that offered graduate students the option of completing a certificate in the pedagogy of their discipline in addition to their Ph.D.'s. However, the prospect of establishing a similar program at KU was daunting: we would need to create and staff formal courses and seek approval from the state board of regents. We realized that for our students, the value did not lie in formal certification, which no college history department would expect, but rather in the documentation of their preparation to teach.

Thus our Commendation in Teaching Preparedness was born. The department issues it to graduate students who have had at least two semesters of experience teaching their own classes, have written a thoughtful statement of teaching philosophy, have taken the practical pedagogy course (History 807), and have participated in the specified number of discussions and workshops of their choice sponsored by the university's Center for Teaching Excellence or the department's Teaching Exchange. In this way, we piggyback our graduate students' pedagogical training on extant noncredit offerings.

Girding for the Job Market. The department already had an established system for helping students in their final year navigate the academic job market. A department placement officer and numerous faculty volunteers help students craft application letters and try out interview skills. The CID made us aware that career planning should start at the beginning of the graduate program rather than in the final year. When students choose their fields of study, we now urge them to think about intellectual coherence and marketability and begin crafting an appealing profile of research, teaching, and service. Each dissertation should have obvious significance and be written for an audience of historians outside of the author's own field because departments rarely duplicate specializations.

Most of all, our department recognized how much students can learn about how the job market works by watching us hire new faculty. Each hiring committee has a graduate student member; students are encouraged to meet candidates, hear their presentations, attend receptions in their honor, review their CVs and publications, and attend department meetings where hiring decisions are made. By the time they reach the job market themselves, attentive students know exactly what to expect.

Are Our Innovations Successful?

Because most of our innovations were enacted in the past two and a half years, we cannot yet know whether they will have the desired impact on our graduates' careers. We have made plans to ascertain how well the new program elements are working by tracking job placement and graduate satisfaction among alumni. These measures, although limited, are well recognized (Maki and Borkowski, 2006).

Initial signs are promising. Time to degree is one recognized marker of graduate program success. Now over 90 percent of graduate students in their first three years are achieving the guidelines of the Progress Grid, which puts them on track to complete their degrees on schedule in five to six years. The first two alumni of our portfolio exam system defended their dissertations in spring 2007, at the end of their fourth year. Both were selected for tenure-track positions at noted universities. Their balanced profile of research, teaching, and professional experience positioned them well to compete in a tight academic job market.

References

Bender, T., Katz, P. M., Palmer, C., and the Committee on Graduate Education of the American Historical Association. *The Education of Historians for the Twenty-First Century.* Urbana: University of Illinois Press, 2004.

Council of Graduate Schools. *Ph.D. Completion and Attrition: Policy, Numbers, Leadership, and Next Steps.* Washington, D.C.: Council of Graduate Schools, 2004.

Golde, C. M. "'Should I Stay or Should I Go?' Student Descriptions of the Doctoral Attrition Process." *Review of Higher Education,* 2000, *23,* 199–227.

Golde, C. M. "The Role of the Department and Discipline in Doctoral Student Attrition: Lessons from Four Departments." *Journal of Higher Education,* 2005, *76,* 669–700.

Golde, C. M., and Dore, T. M. "At Cross Purposes: What the Experiences of Today's Doctoral Students Reveal About Doctoral Education." Philadelphia: Pew Charitable Trusts, 2001. http://www.phd-survey.org/report.htm. Accessed Nov. 30, 2007.

Golde, C. M., and Walker, G. (eds.). *Envisioning the Future of Doctoral Education: Preparing Stewards of the Discipline.* San Francisco: Jossey-Bass, 2006.

Lovitts, B. *Leaving the Ivory Tower: The Causes and Consequences of Departure from Doctoral Study.* Lanham, Md.: Rowman & Littlefield, 2001.

Maki, P. L., and Borkowski, N. A. *The Assessment of Doctoral Education: Emerging Criteria and New Models for Improving Outcomes.* Sterling, Va.: Stylus, 2006.

Nyquist, J. D., and others. "On the Road to Becoming a Professor: The Graduate Student Experience." *Change,* Mar. 1999, 18–27.

EVE LEVIN is a professor in the Department of History at the University of Kansas and its director of graduate studies. A specialist in premodern Russian and eastern European history, she is editor of the journal The Russian Review.

Concluding Thoughts

Carol L. Colbeck, KerryAnn O'Meara, Ann E. Austin

This volume builds on a relatively new but already rich line of research about education for the professoriate. Several of our authors have previously contributed to the growing body of evidence that shows that the intense formal and informal focus on learning to conduct research in doctoral programs leaves future faculty insufficiently prepared for their roles as teachers, academic citizens, and scholars engaged in communities beyond academe.

Most doctoral students, whatever their field of study, still learn what it means to be a professor on a daily basis from watching what faculty do. Perhaps for this reason, the theoretical foundation of much prior research on preparing future faculty has been socialization theory, exploring how doctoral students learn the tasks, attitudes, practices, and values of academic work in general and their disciplines in particular. Socialization theory continues to be very useful, but other theories used by our authors—such as identity theory, a theory of professional apprenticeship, curriculum theories, mentoring theory, and network theory—allow our authors to probe into specific areas of the doctoral student experience, open new avenues for research, and offer new perspectives for improving doctoral education.

These theoretical perspectives speak to each other across the chapters, highlighting nuances of similar themes in new and interesting ways, similar to the way jazz musicians explore variations on musical themes. The themes that play across chapters and theoretical frameworks in this volume include the following:

- Overt and covert messages about faculty work are communicated to doctoral students by faculty, peers, family, and friends—and new doctoral students may interpret those messages in ways that may surprise those who communicate them. (See Chapters Four and Five.)
- The prolonged period of preparation for a faculty career requires formal classroom learning and a structured research apprenticeship appropriate to a student's discipline. It also involves, however, explicit or implicit apprenticeships in ethics, modes of interaction, nature of practice, and prioritization of tasks. (See Chapters Two through Five.)
- Academic work involves more than the discovery, integration, and communication of disciplinary knowledge. As professional work, it requires

New Directions for Teaching and Learning, no. 113, Spring 2008 © Wiley Periodicals, Inc.
Published online in Wiley InterScience (www.interscience.wiley.com) • DOI: 10.1002/tl.311

abilities to deal with unpredictability, complexity, and simultaneous responsibilities to multiple stakeholders with varied interests. (See Chapters One, Two, Three, and Seven.)

- Learning and engaging in professional academic work involves more than taking turns at playing roles defined by others. As doctoral students come to define themselves by one or more academic roles, they assume professional identities. (See Chapters One through Five.)
- Future faculty members' identities may become fragmented to the extent that they believe it is necessary to choose constantly between competing teaching, research, and service identities. They are more likely to develop integrated professional identities, however, if they perceive and use synergies between these identities to address multiple nonroutine, important, and varied issues. (See Chapters One and Three through Six.)

Clearly, applying a variety of theories sheds new light on aspects of the doctoral experience. Expanding our store of theoretical lenses on doctoral education even further will provide new perspectives to researchers as they continue to explore the doctoral experience. A number of research questions remain to be probed. For example, does the process through which professional integration emerges differ across disciplines? What is the long-term impact of some of the strategies discussed, such as CIRTL activities (Chapter Six) and departmental efforts (Chapter Seven)? What does the notion of "integration" come to mean to doctoral graduates whose programs or advisors have been striving to help them develop such a perspective?

In addition to researchers in doctoral education, faculty members, advisors, department chairs, and deans will benefit from lessons learned from new theoretical perspectives as they consider ways to deepen and enrich the doctoral experience. The good news—evident in Chapter Six about interdisciplinary reform in science and engineering and in Chapter Seven about reform in a history department—is that much of the change needed to prepare doctoral students as integrated professionals does not require lots of money. If doctoral students are to become truly integrated professionals, the commitment and imagination of all of current faculty and administrators will be needed to model synergistic connections between research, teaching, and service; to design programs that foster such connections; and to provide opportunities for doctoral students to reflect on their learning. Designing programs and modeling integration, of course, require current faculty to reflect on their own professional practice and sense of identity.

CAROL L. COLBECK *is professor and dean of education at the University of Massachusetts in Boston. Her research investigates how faculty integrate teaching, research, and service; how faculty teaching and organizational climate affect student learning; and how faculty balance professional and personal responsibilities.*

NEW DIRECTIONS FOR TEACHING AND LEARNING • DOI: 10.1002/tl

KERRYANN O'MEARA is associate professor of higher education at the University of Maryland at College Park. Her research focuses on the ways in which we socialize, reward, and support the growth of faculty so that they can make distinct contributions to the goals of higher education.

ANN E. AUSTIN holds the Dr. Mildred B. Erickson Distinguished Chair in Higher, Adult, and Lifelong Education at Michigan State University. Her research focuses on faculty careers and professional development, the preparation of future faculty, teaching and learning issues, academic workplaces, and organizational change and transformation in higher education.

INDEX

AACU (Association of Colleges and Universities), 27, 58
Abbott, A., 13–14, 15
Abes, E., 28
Abrams, D., 65
Academic community, 65
Academic plans, 59, 61–62
Academic profession: benefits of, 9; integrated identities and, 13–14; traits of, 9
Academic work: attention to, 27; changing contexts of, 2–3; in community engagement phases, 30–40; fragmented view of, 44; massive makeover of, 3; as path to academic profession, 9; role labels and, 10; standards of, 90–91
Action research model, 71
Adams, K. A., 1
Adjustment, 59
Admissions, 88–89
Advisory Committee on Graduate Education and American Competitiveness (Council of Graduate Schools), 2–3
Aguirre, A., 31
Alliance for Graduate Education and the Professoriate (AGEP), 1, 44
American Anthropological Association, 34
American Historical Association, 85
Angelo, T. A., 71
Anticipatory stage, 30, 31, 32t, 34
Antonio, A. L., 31
Applications, 96
Apprenticeships: in doctoral education, 21–23; in professional education, 19–21; in traditional preparation programs, 18; types of, 4
Architecture students, 20
Arnold, J., 45
Articulation of identity theory, 11
Arts and sciences programs, 17
Aryee, S., 50
Assessment: of community engagement, 35–36; in professional apprenticeships, 20–21
Association of American Colleges and Universities (AACU), 27, 58
Association of American Universities, 57
Astin, H. S., 31
Attrition, 44

Austin, A. E., 4, 5, 6, 9, 27, 29, 30, 31, 34, 35, 36, 37, 38, 39, 40, 44, 53, 58, 69, 79, 99

Baird, L. L., 31, 37, 50
Barger, S., 76
Barnes, B., 27, 35
Barnett, R. C., 12
Bass, H., 1–2
Bauer, T. N., 44
Beaumont, E., 28
Becker, H. S., 45, 47
Behavior, of students, 59
Bender, T., 85
Bensimon, E. M., 31
Bernstein, D., 85
Bierema, L. L., 45
Bifurcation, of teaching, 1
Bloomgarden, A., 28, 38
Borkowski, N. A., 85, 86, 93, 96
Bouwma-Gearhart, J. L., 66, 76
Braxton, J. M., 11, 31, 37
Brint, S., 15
Brower, R., 15
Brown, J. S., 21
Bucher, R., 47
Burack, C., 37, 38
Burke, P. J., 10, 11, 13
Business students, 48–54

Campus visits, 23
Careerism, 43
Carlson, M., 87
Carnegie Foundation, 4, 18
Carnegie Initiative on the Doctorate (CID), 1, 5, 29, 34, 70, 83, 84–88
Carper, J., 45, 47
Cast, A. D., 9
Center for the Integration of Research, Teaching, and Learning (CIRTL), 5, 29; Delta Program and, 73–78; overview of, 70–73; teaching assistant preparation and, 58, 66–67; Web site for, 78
Chemistry students, 60–66
Citizen-scholars, 2
Clark, B. R., 63
Clarke, S. E., 71
Classical apprenticeship, 19
Classroom Research model, 71
Clifford, M. A., 66, 74, 76

Clinical training, 20
Colbeck, C. L., 1, 4, 5, 6, 9, 11, 12, 13, 14, 15, 28, 31, 38, 40, 43–44, 57, 75, 99
Colby, A., 19, 28
Collins, A., 21
Commitment: to identity, 11–12; to others, 33t, 39–40
Communication, 36
Community engagement: assessment of, 35–36; benefits of, 27; definition of, 28–29; lack of participation in, 28; phases of, 30–40; rationale for, 29; socialization theory and, 30–40; types of, 29
Community-based research methods, 35, 37
Concurrent curricula, 59–60
Connolly, M. R., 5, 66, 74, 76
Content, of curriculum, 59
Conversations, 35
Core courses, 32t, 34–37
Cotton, J. L., 50
Council of Graduate Schools, 2–3, 58, 88
Coursework phase, 34–36
Creating a Collaborative Learning Environment program, 73
Creativity, 3, 62
Cress, C. M., 31
Cross, K. P., 71
Cuban, L., 60
Culture: CIRTL pillars and, 72; in community engagement phases, 37, 39; lack of community involvement and, 28; shared meanings and, 15; using socialization to re-create, 40
Curriculum: in academic plan theory, 59; in concurrent curricula theory, 59–60; deficiencies in, 1; of Delta Program, 73
Curriculum, situated: identity and, 65; overview of, 60; recommendations for, 67–68; sequence of, 63–64

Darrow, C. N., 45
Data, 87
Davis, G., 18
de Janasz, S. C., 46
Degree programs, 91
Delta Program (University of Wisconsin–Madison), 70, 73–79
Developmental networks, 46–47
Dewey, J., 35
Dillenburg, P., 74

Discipline, academic, 2, 35, 79, 90
Discussion groups, 73, 74
Dissertations, 39–40, 93, 94
Diversity, 72–73
Dobrow, S. R., 47, 53
Doctoral preparation: deficiencies in, 1; misalignment of goals and training in, 69; pedagogies of practice in, 21–23; versus professional education, 19–20; traditional types of, 17–19
Doctoral students: career desires of, 29; common complaints of, 1; developmental stages of, 30; first semester experiences of, 44–45, 48–54
Documentation, of work, 38
Doing, ways of, 62–63
Dole Institute, 87
Dore, T. M., 1, 18, 29, 69, 86
Dougherty, T. W., 45
Dreher, G. F., 45
Driscoll, A., 28, 29, 38
Duguid, P., 21

Economic competitiveness, 2–3
Education: schools of, 20, 22; versus training, 61–62
Education of Historians for the Twenty-First Century (Bender, Katz, Palmer, and the Committee on Graduate Education of the American Historical Association), 85
Ehrlich Award, 28
Ehrlich, T., 28
Eisenhardt, K. M., 48
Eisner, E. W., 58, 59
Electives, 95
Elkana, Y., 14
Elman, S. E., 28
Employers, 79, 91, 96
Energy, 11–12, 13
English majors, 22
Entrepreneurial spirit, 38
Epstein, S., 90
Ethics: apprenticeships and, 19, 21; in community engagement phases, 35, 36; pedagogies of practice and, 23
Evaluation: in academic plan theory, 59; in concurrent curricula theory, 59; of training models, 75; of University of Kansas History Department, 90–91
Exams, 93
Expeditions in Learning program, 73
Experiential education, 35
Expertise, 13

Extra curricula, 59
Eyler, J., 35

Faculty: community engagement efforts of, 28; out-of-discipline work and, 79; requirements of, 23; retirement of, 17, 29; rewards of work for, 52; shadowing of, 23; in teaching assistant preparation study, 61–66
Faculty, new: expectations of, 18, 38–39; fragmentation of work and, 53; integrated identities of, 13–14
Feedback, 64
Financial issues, 38
Finkelstein, M. J., 3, 4, 12, 44
Foreign language, 92
Formal stage, 30, 32t, 34
Fragmentation, of roles, 43–54, 57
Friedson, E., 14, 15
Funding innovations, 88–89

Gaff, J. G., 1, 18, 27, 58, 70
Gherardi, S., 58, 60, 63, 65
Giles, D. E., 35
Goals, of programs, 69
Golde, C., 1, 4, 17, 18, 29, 34, 44, 50, 69, 85, 86, 88, 89
Graduate students. See Doctoral students
Graduate studies. See Academic work
Grants, 38
Green, S. G., 44, 50
Greenwood, E., 9
Grossman, P., 20

Hartley, M., 28
Hidden curricula, 59, 62, 64, 65
Higgins, M. C., 46, 47, 53
Hirsch, D., 37, 38
Historians, 86
History, of institution, 35
Hoffer, T. B., 1
Hogg, M. A., 65
Hollander, E., 28
Howard University, 72
Huber, M. T., 43
Huberman, A. M., 49
Humanities departments, 22
Hutchings, P., 29, 71
Hyde, J. S., 12

Ibarra, H., 9, 46, 47, 53
Identity: challenges of, 10–12; definition of, 10; situated learning and, 65
Identity apprenticeship, 19, 21, 23

Identity development: in community engagement phases, 34; multiple identities and, 10–13; need for, 9; recommendations regarding, 14–15; relationships and, 45–47; role labels and, 10
Informal stage, 30, 33t, 38–39
Institutional missions, 40
Instructional processes, 59
Instructional resources, 59
Integrated approach. See Role integration
Integrative skills, 38
Intellectual apprenticeships, 19, 20, 22
Intended curricula, 59, 63
International context, of academic work, 2–3
Internships, 73–74, 77
Interpersonal skills, 36
Interview skills, 96
Introductory seminars, 31, 34
Investment, 30, 33t
Involvement, 30, 33t
Isabella, L. A., 45

Jackson, G., 28
Jackson, P. W., 59
Janke, E. M., 5, 57
Job market, 96
Johnson, K., 45
Jones, S., 28
Journals, 38, 93

Kadushin, C., 46
Katz, P. M., 85
Kaufmann, J. B., 48
Kennedy, D., 18
Kilduff, M., 46, 47
Kirkpatrick, D. L., 75
Klay, W. E., 15
Klein, E. B., 45
Knowing, ways of, 62–63
Knowledge acquisition, 30, 32t, 34–36, 37
Kolb, D., 35
Kraimer, M. L., 46
Kram, K., 45, 46, 47
Kwiram, A. L., 58

Labor, division of, 13–14
Laboratory learning, 21–22, 23
Lattuca, L. R., 15, 58, 59, 61
Law schools, 20
Learned curricula, 59–60
Learners, 59, 63
Learning Communities (LC) pillar, 71–72

Learning through-Diversity (LTD) pillar,
    71, 72
Levin, E., 5
Levinson, D. J., 45
Levinson, M. A., 45
Lewin, T., 84
Liden, R. C., 46
Lovitts, B., 69, 88
Lower-status faculty, 14
Lynton Award, 28
Lynton, E., 28, 29, 38

Maki, P. L., 85, 86, 93, 96
Managerial skills, 37–38
Manuscript preparation, 23
Margaret Mead Award, 34
Margolis, E., 59
Marketing programs, 31, 32t, 34
Marks, S. R., 11, 12
Mastery development, 33t, 37–39
McAfee, N, 37
McDaniels, M., 4, 9, 27, 29, 30, 31, 34,
    36, 37, 38, 39, 40
McKee, B., 45
Medical field, 19, 20, 21–22
Mentoring theory, 45–47
Mentors: in community engagement
    phases, 35, 38, 40; in Delta Program,
    73; doctoral student experience and,
    48–54; effective versus ineffective, 58;
    innovations for, 89–90; in teaching
    assistant preparation, 58, 66; in tradi-
    tional preparation programs, 18
Merriam, S. B., 45
Michael, P., 28, 31, 40
Michigan State University, 70, 72
Miles, M. B., 49
Military officers, 84
Millar, S. B., 74, 76
Minority faculty, 31
Multiple identities, 10–13

Nardi, P. M., 30, 39
National Research Council, 84
National Science Foundation, 5, 58, 70,
    73
Networking: current study of, 44–45,
    48–54; doctoral students' perspectives
    of work and, 51–52; mentoring theory
    and, 45–47, 50; as part of community
    engagement phases, 38; prior studies
    of, 44; professional identity and, 47,
    50–52; social networks theory and,
    46–47, 50
Nicolini, D., 58, 60, 63, 65

Nontraditional students, 84
Null curricula, 59, 63
Nyquist, J. D., 23, 44, 69, 79, 86

Observational learning, 18, 20, 21, 63
Odella, F., 58, 60, 63, 65
Official curricula, 59
Older academic professional model, 1
O'Meara, K., 4, 6, 13, 27, 28, 29, 36, 38,
    99
Oral exams, 94
Orientation: in community engagement
    program, 31, 32t, 34; doctoral stu-
    dents' perceived messages from, 48–
    52; to professions, 36–37
Osmosis theory, 18

Palmer, C., 85
The Paper Chase (film), 19
Participatory action, 35
Pedagogical strategies: in community
    engagement phases, 35, 36; in Delta
    Program training, 76–77; in doctoral
    education, 21–23; professional appren-
    ticeships and, 19–21; questions to con-
    sider in, 23–24; in teaching assistant
    preparation, 66; in traditional prepara-
    tion programs, 18–19; in University of
    Kansas History Department program,
    95
Peer relationships, 44, 45
Pennsylvania State University, 70, 72
Personal qualities, 47
Personal stage, 30, 33t
PFF (Preparing Future Faculty) pro-
    gram, 1, 27, 44, 58, 70
Pfund, C., 76
Portfolios, 93–94
Posner, G. J., 58, 59, 61, 63, 64
Postdoctoral positions, 18
Practice, 63, 64
Pratt, M. G., 48
Preparation for the Professions Program
    (PPP), 18–19
Preparing Future Faculty (PFF) pro-
    gram, 1, 27, 44, 58, 70
Problem solving, 62
Productivity, 13
Profession: activities in, 91–92; defini-
    tion of, 2; division of labor in, 13–14;
    integrated identities and, 13–14
Professional communities, 38
Professional development, 62, 76, 78–79,
    95
Professional education, 18, 19–21

Professional essays, 94
Professional identity, 45–47, 50–54
Professional orientations, 36–37
Progress Grid evaluation, 90–91
Provisional selves, 47
Pruitt-Logan, A. S., 1, 27, 58, 70
Public good, 3
Publications: apprenticeships and, 23; careerism and, 43; first-semester doctoral students' perceptions of, 49; innovations in, 92–93; reward of, 52
Purpose, of curriculum, 59, 61

Quality, of instruction, 18

Ragins, B. R., 50
Reason, P., 71
Recruiting students, 32, 32t, 34
Reflection, 21, 23, 35
Reforms, 1, 2–3
Reis, R. M., 18
Relationship constellation, 46
Relationships. See specific types
Research: CIRTL principles and, 71; in community engagement phases, 35–37; faculty rewards and, 52; incoming graduate students' perceptions of, 49–50, 51, 53; multiple identities and, 12; pedagogies of practice in, 21–22, 23; teaching assistants' perception of, 63–67
Research assistants, 51
Research institutions, 43, 44
Research seminars, 92–93
Resource acquisition, 38
Responsive Ph.D. project, 29
Retirement, faculty, 17, 29
Reward systems: as barrier to community engagement, 28; careerism and, 43; in community engagement phases, 38; fragmentation and, 52; in University of Kansas History Department, 95–96
Rhoades, G., 1, 13, 34
Rhoads, R. A., 13
Rice, R. E., 1, 27, 29
Risk taking, 63–64
Robinson, B., 87
Rockman, K. W., 48
Role acquisition, 34, 38
Role fragmentation, 43–54, 57
Role integration: benefits of, 2; definition of, 57; in Delta Program, 73–78; goals of, 2–3; multiple identities and, 11–13; overview of, 1; rationale for, 3; teaching assistants and, 66–67

Role labels, 10
Romero, M., 59
Routine work, 13–14

Salience, of identity, 11
Schein, E. H., 47, 53
Scholarship of Teaching and Learning model, 71
Schuster, J. H., 3, 4, 12, 44
Science, technology, engineering, and mathematics (STEM) students, 58; CIRTL's mission and, 70; CIRTL's principles and, 71; Delta Program for, 73–78
Scott, W. R., 1, 13
Seibert, S. E., 46
Selection committees, 35
Seminars, 92–93
Sequence, curriculum, 59, 63–64
Service awards, 34
Service-learning: marketing of, 31; pedagogy of, 35; in undergraduate programs, 29
Shadowing faculty, 23
Shared meanings, 11, 12, 15
Shulenburger, D., 84
Shulman, L. S., 29
Silva, M. K., 9
Simulations, 20
Singleton, S., 37, 38
Situated curriculum: identity and, 65; overview of, 60; recommendations for, 67–68; sequence of, 63–64
Skill apprenticeship: definition of, 19; example of, 20–21; pedagogies of practice in, 23
Smallwood, S., 44
Smock, S. M., 28
Social compact, 3
Social networks theory, 46–47
Socialization theory: community engagement and, 30–40; continued use of, 99; in faculty preparation research, 4; overview of, 29–30
Socializing students, 30–40, 65
Solon T. Kimball Award for Public and Applied Anthropology, 34
Sorcinelli, M. D., 29
Spouses, of doctoral students, 50
Sprague, J., 44, 69, 79
Staff management, 37–38
Stanton, T. K., 29
Stark, J. S., 58, 59, 61
Steadman, M., 71
Stein, E. L., 30, 31, 34, 38, 39, 44

Stelling, J. G, 47
STEM. *See* Science, technology, engineering, and mathematics students
Stephens, J., 28
Stereotypes, 63
Stone, R., 50
Strand, K., 35, 36, 37
Stress, 10–11
Strikwerda, C., 84, 85
Stringer, E., 71
Stryker, S., 10, 11
Student-advisor relationship: influence of, 50; innovations in, 89–90; prior research regarding, 44
Students. *See* Doctoral students
Student-student relationships, 44, 50
Sullivan, S. E., 46
Sullivan, W. M., 3, 4, 19, 20, 21
Surveys, 85–86
Sweitzer, V. L., 5, 43
Syllabus, 90

Tacit knowledge, 18
Tajfel, H., 65
TAR (Teaching-as-Research) pillar, 71, 73, 77
Taught curricula, 59
Teacher preparation programs, 20, 22
Teaching: CIRTL principles and, 71; as focus of teaching assistant programs, 62; graduate students' perceptions of, 49–50, 51–52; rewards of, 52; students' limited experiences with, 74; teaching assistants' perception of, 63–67; University of Kansas innovations in, 94–96
Teaching assistants: current practices for preparing, 58; funding innovations for, 88; in humanities departments, 22; reduction of fragmentation and, 44; role integration of, 66–67; study of preparation program for, 60–66; teaching perceptions of, 63–67; in University of Kansas History Department, 94
Teaching-as-Research (TAR) pillar, 71, 73, 77
Tenure-track positions, 12, 43–44
Term-limited appointments, 3
Tested curricula, 59
Texas A&M University, 72
Theology students, 20
Thesis, 92
Thoits, P. A., 12
Thomas, D. A., 46

Thornton, R., 30, 39
Tierney, W. G., 28, 31, 34, 40
Time pressures, 11–12
Tinto, V., 44
Training: in Delta Program, 73–78; versus education, 61–62; evaluation model for, 75; misalignment of goals and, 69; ways of knowing versus ways of doing in, 62–63
Tsai, W., 46, 47
Turner, J. C., 65
Twale, D. J., 30, 31, 34, 38, 39, 44

Undergraduate programs, 29, 31
University of Colorado at Boulder, 72
University of Kansas History Department: evaluation of change at, 96–97; innovations at, 86–96; myths about Carnegie Initiative at, 84–86; overview of, 83–84
University of Wisconsin–Madison Delta Program, 70, 73–78
U.S. News and World Report, 84

Values, personal, 36–37, 38–39
Van Emmerick, I.J.H., 46
Vanderbilt University, 72

Wagner, J. W., 29
Walker, G., 29, 34, 70, 85
Walshok, M. L., 37
Ward, K., 28
Webb, N., 76
Weibl, R. A., 1
Weidman, J. C., 30, 31, 34, 38, 39, 44
Weisbuch, R., 29, 70
Well-being, 12
Wellman, B., 46
Whitely, W., 45
Whiting, V., 46
Williams, B., 15
Women, 31
Woodrow Wilson Foundation's Responsive Ph.D. Program, 70
Work and Integrity (Sullivan), 19
Work, identifying with, 47
Workers, versus learners, 63
Worster, D., 93
Wulff, D. H., 44, 53, 58, 69, 79
Wyatt, T, 50

Yin, R. K., 49

Zlotkowski, E., 28

TL112   **Curriculum Development in Higher Education: Faculty-Driven Processes and Practices**
Peter Wolf, Julia Christensen Hughes
Faculty within institutions of higher education are increasingly being asked to play leadership roles in curriculum assessment and reform initiatives. This change is being driven by quality concerns; burgeoning disciplinary knowledge; interest in a broader array of learning outcomes, including skills and values; and growing support for constructivist pedagogies and learning-centered, interdisciplinary curricula. It is essential that faculty be well prepared to take a scholarly approach to this work. To that end, this issue of *New Directions for Teaching and Learning* presents the frameworks used and lessons learned by faculty, administrators, and educational developers in a variety of curriculum assessment and development processes. Collectively, the authors in this volume present the context and catalysts of higher education curriculum reform, advocate for the Scholarship of Curriculum Practice (SoCP), provide examples of curricular assessment and development initiatives at a variety of institutional levels, suggest that educational developers can provide much support to such processes, and argue that this work has profound implications for the faculty role. Anyone involved in curriculum assessment and development will find food for thought in each chapter.
ISBN 978-04702-78512

TL111   **Scholarship of Multicultural Teaching and Learning**
Matthew Kaplan, A.T. Miller
Because effective approaches to multicultural teaching and learning are still being developed in institutions across the U.S. and around the world, it is essential to study and document promising practices. It is only through rigorous research and comparative studies that we can be assured that the significant investments many institutions are making in multicultural education for the development of individual student and faculty skills, and the overall betterment of society, will reap positive results. This volume of *New Directions for Teaching and Learning* provides the valuable results of such research as well as models for the types of research that others could carry out in this area. The volume will appeal to new and experienced practitioners of multicultural teaching. It offers documented illustrations of how such teaching is designed, carried out, and is effective in varied higher education contexts and in a wide range of disciplines representing the humanities, social sciences, engineering and math, and the arts.
ISBN 978-04702-23826

TL110   **Neither White Nor Male: Female Faculty of Color**
Katherine Grace Hendrix
Given limited information on the academic experience in general and on the pedagogical strategies and strengths of faculty of color in particular, the scholars in this issue have come together to begin the process of articulating the academic experiences of female professors of color. While chronicling our challenges within academia as well as our contributions to the education of U.S. students, this collaborative effort will add depth to the existing literature on faculty of color, serve as a reference for positioning women of color within the larger context of higher education (moving us from the

margin to the center), and lay a foundation for more inclusive future research.
ISBN: 04702-2382-6

TL109   **Self-Authorship: Advancing Students' Intellectual Growth**
Peggy S. Meszaros
This issue addresses the limitations of national efforts to focus students' intellectual development narrowly on testing and explores why educators in higher education should consider using the lens of self-authorship and the Learning Partnerships Model for a more holistic model of student intellectual development. The chapters provide examples of institutional transformations needed to support change in teaching and learning and examples of assessment, research, and curricular development based in self-authorship theory. The summary chapter by Marcia Baxter Magolda ties the themes from each of the chapters together and offers promise for the future. The final chapter provides ideas for next steps in promoting the use of self-authorship to advance the intellectual development of college students. The audience for this volume is broad, ranging from college faculty to student affairs faculty and staff to college administrators who are facing assessment challenges for reporting student learning outcomes to their various consti-tuencies, agencies, and boards. This volume should also prove instructive to faculty embarking on curriculum revisions and identifying and measuring student learning outcomes for undergraduate and graduate students.
ISBN: 07879-9721-2

TL108   **Developing Student Expertise and Community: Lessons from How People Learn**
Anthony J. Petrosino, Taylor Martin, Vanessa Svihla
This issue presents research from a collaboration among learning scientists, assessment experts, technologists, and subject-matter experts, with the goal of producing adaptive expertise in students. The model is based on the National Research Council book *How People Learn*. The chapters present case studies of working together to develop learning environments centered on challenge-based instruction. While the strategies and research come from engineering, they are applicable across disciplines to help students think about the process of problem solving.
ISBN: 07879-9574-6

TL107   **Exploring Research-Based Teaching**
Carolin Kreber
Investigates the wide scope research-based teaching, while focusing on two distinct forms. The first sees research-based teaching as student-focused, inquiry-based learning; students become generators of knowledge. The second perspective fixes the lens on teachers; the teaching is characterized by discipline-specific inquiry into the teaching process itself. Both methods have positive effects on student learning, and this volume explores research and case studies.
ISBN: 07879-9077-9

TL106   **Supplemental Instruction: New Visions for Empowering Student Learning**
Marion E. Stone, Glen Jacobs
Supplemental Instruction (SI) is an academic support model introduced over thirty years ago to help students be successful in difficult courses. SI teaches students how to learn via regularly scheduled, out-of-class collaborative sessions with other students. This volume both introduces the tenets of SI to beginners and brings those familiar up to speed with today's methods and the future directions. Includes case studies, how-to's, benefits to students and faculty, and more.
ISBN: 0-7879-8680-1

TL105 **A Laboratory for Public Scholarship and Democracy**
Rosa A. Eberly, Jeremy Cohen
Public scholarship has grown out of the scholarship-and-service model, but its end is democracy rather than volunteerism. The academy has intellectual and creative resources that can help build involved, democratic communities through public scholarship. Chapters present concepts, processes, and case studies from Penn State's experience with public scholarship.
ISBN: 0-7879-8530-9

TL104 **Spirituality in Higher Education**
Sherry L. Hoppe, Bruce W. Speck
With chapters by faculty and administrators, this book investigates the role of spirituality in educating the whole student while recognizing that how spirituality is viewed, taught, and experienced is intensely personal. The goal is not to prescribe a method for integrating spirituality but to offer options and perspectives. Readers will be reminded that the quest for truth and meaning, not the destination, is what is vitally important.
ISBN: 0-7879-8363-2

TL103 **Identity, Learning, and the Liberal Arts**
Ned Scott Laff
Argues that we must foster conversations between liberal studies and student development theory, because the skills inherent in liberal learning are the same skills used for personal development. Students need to experience core learning that truly influences their critical thinking skills, character development, and ethics. Educators need to design student learning encounters that develop these areas. This volume gives examples of how liberal arts education can be a healthy foundation for life skills.
ISBN: 0-7879-8333-0

TL102 **Advancing Faculty Learning Through Interdisciplinary Collaboration**
Elizabeth G. Creamer, Lisa R. Lattuca
Explores why stakeholders in higher education should refocus attention on collaboration as a form of faculty learning. Chapters give theoretical basis then practical case studies for collaboration's benefits in outreach, scholarship, and teaching. Also discusses impacts on education policy, faculty hiring and development, and assessment of collaborative work.
ISBN: 0-7879-8070-6

TL101 **Enhancing Learning with Laptops in the Classroom**
Linda B. Nilson, Barbara E. Weaver
This volume contains case studies—mostly from Clemson University's leading-edge laptop program—that address victories as well as glitches in teaching with laptop computers in the classroom. Disciplines using laptops include psychology, music, statistics, animal sciences, and humanities. The volume also advises faculty on making a laptop mandate successful at their university, with practical guidance for both pedagogy and student learning.
ISBN: 0-7879-8049-8

TL100 **Alternative Strategies for Evaluating Student Learning**
Michelle V. Achacoso, Marilla D. Svinicki
Teaching methods are adapting to the modern era, but innovation in assessment of student learning lags behind. This volume examines theory and practical examples of creative new methods of evaluation, including authentic testing, testing with multimedia, portfolios, group exams, visual synthesis, and performance-based testing. Also investigates improving students' ability to take and learn from tests, before and after.
ISBN: 0-7879-7970-8

TL99   Addressing Faculty and Student Classroom Improprieties
John M. Braxton, Alan E. Bayer
Covers the results of a large research study on occurrence and perceptions of classroom improprieties by both students and faculty. When classroom norms are violated, all parties in a classroom are affected, and teaching and learning suffer. The authors offer guidelines for both student and faculty classroom behavior and how institutions might implement those suggestions.
ISBN: 0-7879-7794-2

TL98   Decoding the Disciplines: Helping Students Learn Disciplinary Ways of Thinking
David Pace, Joan Middendorf
The Decoding the Disciplines model is a way to teach students the critical-thinking skills required to understand their specific discipline. Faculty define bottlenecks to learning, dissect the ways experts deal with the problematic issues, and invent ways to model experts' thinking for students. Chapters are written by faculty in diverse fields who successfully used these methods and became involved in the scholarship of teaching and learning.
ISBN: 0-7879-7789-6

TL97   Building Faculty Learning Communities
Milton D. Cox, Laurie Richlin
A very effective way to address institutional challenges is a faculty learning community. FLCs are useful for preparing future faculty, reinvigorating senior faculty, and implementing new courses, curricula, or campus initiatives. The results of FLCs parallel those of student learning communities, such as retention, deeper learning, respect for others, and greater civic participation. This volume describes FLCs from a practitioner's perspective, with plenty of advice, wisdom, and lessons for starting your own FLC.
ISBN: 0-7879-7568-0

TL96   Online Student Ratings of Instruction
Trav D. Johnson, D. Lynn Sorenson
Many institutions are adopting Web-based student ratings of instruction, or are considering doing it, because online systems have the potential to save time and money among other benefits. But they also present a number of challenges. The authors of this volume have firsthand experience with electronic ratings of instruction. They identify the advantages, consider costs and benefits, explain their solutions, and provide recommendations on how to facilitate online ratings.
ISBN: 0-7879-7262-2

TL95   Problem-Based Learning in the Information Age
Dave S. Knowlton, David C. Sharp
Provides information about theories and practices associated with problem-based learning, a pedagogy that allows students to become more engaged in their own education by actively interpreting information. Today's professors are adopting problem-based learning across all disciplines to faciliate a broader, modern definition of what it means to learn. Authors provide practical experience about designing useful problems, creating conducive learning environments, facilitating students' activities, and assessing students' efforts at problem solving.
ISBN: 0-7879-7172-3

TL94   **Technology: Taking the Distance out of Learning**
Margit Misangyi Watts
This volume addresses the possibilities and challenges of computer
technology in higher education. The contributors examine the pressures to
use technology, the reasons not to, the benefits of it, the feeling of being a
learner as well as a teacher, the role of distance education, and the place of
computers in the modern world. Rather than discussing only specific
successes or failures, this issue addresses computers as a new cultural
symbol and begins meaningful conversations about technology in general
and how it affects education in particular.
ISBN: 0-7879-6989-3

TL93   **Valuing and Supporting Undergraduate Research**
Joyce Kinkead
The authors gathered in this volume share a deep belief in the value of
undergraduate research. Research helps students develop skills in problem
solving, critical thinking, and communication, and undergraduate
researchers' work can contribute to an institution's quest to further
knowledge and help meet societal challenges. Chapters provide an overview
of undergraduate research, explore programs at different types of
institutions, and offer suggestions on how faculty members can find ways to
work with undergraduate researchers.
ISBN: 0-7879-6907-9

TL92   **The Importance of Physical Space in Creating Supportive Learning
Environments**
Nancy Van Note Chism, Deborah J. Bickford
The lack of extensive dialogue on the importance of learning spaces in
higher education environments prompted the essays in this volume. Chapter
authors look at the topic of learning spaces from a variety of perspectives,
elaborating on the relationship between physical space and learning, arguing
for an expanded notion of the concept of learning spaces and furnishings,
talking about the context within which decision making for learning spaces
takes place, and discussing promising approaches to the renovation of old
learning spaces and the construction of new ones.
ISBN: 0-7879-6344-5

TL91   **Assessment Strategies for the On-Line Class: From Theory to Practice**
Rebecca S. Anderson, John F. Bauer, Bruce W. Speck
Addresses the kinds of questions that instructors need to ask themselves as
they begin to move at least part of their students' work to an on-line format.
Presents an initial overview of the need for evaluating students' on-line work
with the same care that instructors give to the work in hard-copy format.
Helps guide instructors who are considering using on-line learning in
conjunction with their regular classes, as well as those interested in going
totally on-line.
ISBN: 0-7879-6343-7

TL90   **Scholarship in the Postmodern Era: New Venues, New Values, New
Visions**
Kenneth J. Zahorski
A little over a decade ago, Ernest Boyer's *Scholarship Reconsidered* burst upon
the academic scene, igniting a robust national conversation that maintains
its vitality to this day. This volume aims at advancing that important
conversation. Its first section focuses on the new settings and circumstances

in which the act of scholarship is being played out; its second identifies and explores the fresh set of values currently informing today's scholarly practices; and its third looks to the future of scholarship, identifying trends, causative factors, and potentialities that promise to shape scholars and their scholarship in the new millennium.
ISBN: 0-7879-6293-7

TL89   **Applying the Science of Learning to University Teaching and Beyond**
Diane F. Halpern, Milton D. Hakel
Seeks to build on empirically validated learning activities to enhance what and how much is learned and how well and how long it is remembered. Demonstrates that the movement for a real science of learning—the application of scientific principles to the study of learning—has taken hold both under the controlled conditions of the laboratory and in the messy real-world settings where most of us go about the business of teaching and learning.
ISBN: 0-7879-5791-7

TL88   **Fresh Approaches to the Evaluation of Teaching**
Christopher Knapper, Patricia Cranton
Describes a number of alternative approaches, including interpretive and critical evaluation, use of teaching portfolios and teaching awards, performance indicators and learning outcomes, technology-mediated evaluation systems, and the role of teacher accreditation and teaching scholarship in instructional evaluation.
ISBN: 0-7879-5789-5

TL87   **Techniques and Strategies for Interpreting Student Evaluations**
Karron G. Lewis
Focuses on all phases of the student rating process—from data-gathering methods to presentation of results. Topics include methods of encouraging meaningful evaluations, mid-semester feedback, uses of quality teams and focus groups, and creating questions that target individual faculty needs and interest.
ISBN: 0-7879-5789-5

TL86   **Scholarship Revisited: Perspectives on the Scholarship of Teaching**
Carolin Kreber
Presents the outcomes of a Delphi Study conducted by an international panel of academics working in faculty evaluation scholarship and postsecondary teaching and learning. Identifies the important components of scholarship of teaching, defines its characteristics and outcomes, and explores its most pressing issues.
ISBN: 0-7879-5447-0

TL85   **Beyond Teaching to Mentoring**
Alice G. Reinarz, Eric R. White
Offers guidelines to optimizing student learning through classroom activities as well as peer, faculty, and professional mentoring. Addresses mentoring techniques in technical training, undergraduate business, science, and liberal arts studies, health professions, international study, and interdisciplinary work.
ISBN: 0-7879-5617-1

New Directions for Teaching and Learning
Order Form
SUBSCRIPTIONS AND SINGLE ISSUES

SUBSCRIPTIONS: *(1 year, 4 issues)*

☐ New Order   ☐ Renewal

U.S.	☐ Individual: $80	☐ Institutional: $195
Canada/Mexico	☐ Individual: $80	☐ Institutional: $235
All Others	☐ Individual: $104	☐ Institutional: $269

Call 888-378-2537 or see mailing and pricing instructions below. Online subscriptions are available at www.interscience.wiley.com.

Copy or detach page and send to:
John Wiley & Sons, Journals Dept, 5th Floor
989 Market Street, San Francisco, CA 94103-1741

Order Form can also be faxed to: 888-481-2665

Issue/Subscription Amount: $ _____	**SHIPPING CHARGES:**
Shipping Amount: $ _____	SURFACE Domestic Canadian
(for single issues only—subscription prices include shipping)	First Item $5.00 $6.00
Total Amount: $ _____	Each Add'l Item $3.00 $1.50

(No sales tax for U.S. subscriptions. Canadian residents, add GST for subscription orders. Individual rate subscriptions must be paid by personal check or credit card. Individual rate subscriptions may not be resold as library copies.)

☐ Payment enclosed (U.S. check or money order only. All payments must be in U.S. dollars.)

☐ VISA ☐ MC ☐ Amex # _____ Exp. Date _____

Card Holder Name _____ Card Issue # _____

Signature _____ Day Phone _____

☐ Bill Me (U.S. institutional orders only. Purchase order required.)

Purchase order # _____
Federal Tax ID13559302   GST 89102 8052

Name _____

Address _____

Phone _____ E-mail _____

JB7ND